UNTIL HE COMES

UNDERSTANDING THE END-TIME PRAYER MOVEMENT

Billy Humphrey

forerunner
PUBLISHING

International House of Prayer Missions Base, Kansas City
IHOP.org

forerunner
PUBLISHING

Until He Comes: Understanding the End-Time Prayer Movement
By Billy Humphrey

Published by Forerunner Publishing
International House of Prayer
3535 E. Red Bridge Road
Kansas City, MO 64137
forerunnerpublishing@ihop.org
IHOP.org

ISBN: 978-0-9823262-3-7

Cover art by Seth Parks
Printed in the United States of America

TABLE OF CONTENTS

DEDICATION

To my sons Evan, Siah, and Coby: You are forerunners living at the end of the age! I pray this book will give you understanding of the global end-time prayer movement. You are the love of my life.

ENDORSEMENTS

Billy Humphrey has written an important resource for the Praying Church. *Until He Comes* takes you on a journey through the Scriptures to offer a clear biblical basis for night and day prayer, as well as prophetic insight into God's end-time agenda for the prayer movement that is sweeping the globe. I recommend it to anyone whose heart is being stirred to pursue the Lord in prayer and fasting in this hour.

—Mike Bickle, director of the International House of Prayer of Kansas City

The rumblings are everywhere. A surge of corporate prayer is exploding globally. Believers worldwide are asking questions like, 'What's happening? Is it scriptural? Where is it going? Why should I get involved?' This is possibly the first book written specifically to answer these questions, and Billy Humphrey has the credentials to address them. A weighty book, released at a critical hour.

—Bob Sorge, author, *Secrets of the Secret Place*

I am convinced we live in the greatest hour of history. The glory of the Lord is rising on the Church and her light is shining brightly in the midst of darkness. God's heart longs for nations, and He is intent on giving His Son the inheritance He asked for. Because of this, God is on the move and stirring His people to give themselves fully to what He is doing in the earth. At the forefront of what God is doing is a global prayer movement rumbling through the nations. Night and day prayer is arising to God from every corner of the earth. Billy Humphrey is a modern-day revivalist who has given himself to a life of prayer and answered the high call of God to stand with Jesus in intercession. Billy's mandate to call people to a life of night and day prayer is not coming out of a theory, but has been birthed in the prayer room. In *Until He Comes*, Billy expresses his mandate by calling us to engage in the global prayer movement. Billy's contribution to the worldwide prayer movement is unmistakable, and his passion for the heart of God is unquestionable.

—Banning Liebscher, Jesus Culture Director at
   Bethel Church, Redding, CA

Billy Humphrey has been branded by heaven with a vision for day and night prayer, and he makes a compelling case through Scripture and history that this is God's plan. My heart was stirred to live more deeply in the secret place as I absorbed the fresh, faith-building challenge of this book.

—Dr. Michael L. Brown, President, FIRE School of
   Ministry, Concord, NC

ACKNOWLEDGMENTS

I want to thank Mike Bickle and Lou Engle for blazing a trail in prayer that is challenging an entire generation to wholeheartedly pursue the Lord. I greatly appreciate their friendship and encouragement.

I am grateful to Bob Sorge for exhorting me to develop as a writer—for motivating me to stretch myself and continue to grow.

I want to thank Jono Hall for his input on the chapter "Historical Accounts of Night and Day Prayer." His research and writing have helped shape what I have written.

I want to thank Jamie Burns, Jules Tompkins, and Lisa Garcia for their efforts in helping me write this book. Their input, suggestions, and research on this project have greatly improved this work. Without their help, this book would not have become a reality.

I want to thank Jennifer Sansom for her masterful editing. Her skill and insight were invaluable in sculpting the final manuscript.

FOREWORD

In 1993, I read an article on prayer that prophesied that the Lord was going to raise up twenty-four-hour houses of prayer throughout the earth. The Lord gripped my heart with this vision. Three years later, He clearly told me to pray for the "Moravian Lampstand" to be re-commissioned. For 120 years, the fire of night and day prayer burned in Herrnhut, Germany through a band of Moravian believers

The Lord later spoke clearly to us at TheCall, a prayer ministry I helped found. He said in a dream, "Wherever TheCall goes, I will establish My house of prayer." It is not enough to simply have breakthrough prayer meetings; we must sustain what we gain spiritually with continuous intercession and worship.

Now, over a decade later, I burn with anticipation as we are witnessing God begin to fulfill His prophetic promises. He is rekindling the flame of prayer that the Moravians carried for over a century. All over the world, God is establishing houses of prayer built on uninterrupted intercession and worship.

I am convinced that 24/7 prayer is the necessary precursor to the greatest awakening the earth will ever see. A global fasting and prayer movement is rapidly gaining momentum—entire nations are being mobilized to cry out in intercession. What could be the outcome but an incredible harvest of souls and the return of the Lord Jesus Himself?

Until He Comes is an invaluable resource to the Church. In this book, Billy Humphrey calls believers to follow in the footsteps of the prolific intercessors from the Bible as well as from church history.

I highly recommend *Until He Comes* to anyone who is interested in the global prayer movement. You will be challenged to rethink your understanding of prayer and provoked to respond to the call of Joel 2 with fasting, weeping, and mourning.

I pray that you will be part of this restoration and that your heart will be set ablaze with God's vision for night and day prayer in this generation so that we might truly see the prayer of Jesus answered: "Your kingdom come. Your will be done, on earth as it is in heaven" (Mt. 6:10).

Lou Engle
TheCall, Inc.

INTRODUCTION

In the fall of 2003, after I had served as a youth pastor for thirteen years, the Lord moved my family and me to Kansas City, Missouri. God had given us a vision to plant a house of prayer in Atlanta, so we went to Kansas City to learn the message and model of the International House of Prayer.

After a short period of time at IHOP–KC, it became evident to me that I lacked a biblical theology of prayer. I also lacked understanding of the purpose and scriptural precedents for praying night and day. I was captivated by the concept, but had no biblical or historical foundation for it. So I went on a journey to find out what the Bible said about night and day prayer. If I was to lead a 24/7 prayer ministry, it was probably a good idea to find out if the concept was biblically supported!

After studying the relevant scriptures, not only did I find ample support for night and day prayer, I found that night and day prayer is a continuous reality from Genesis to Revelation. I also saw from Scripture how God would use a massive prayer movement to finalize this age and bring His kingdom to earth. These truths ignited my heart as zeal for His house began to consume me.

We returned to Atlanta in the fall of 2004 to find God's great favor awaiting us. We planted IHOP–Atlanta, and many gathered to engage in ceaseless intercessory worship. Within eighteen months, we extended the prayer meetings to cover twenty-four hours a day, seven days a week. By God's grace we have continued the worship-led prayer meetings to this day.

As you can imagine, planting a missions base that has 24/7 prayer as its centerpiece causes many questions to arise. "What is it you guys do again?" "Where is that in the Bible?" And as one pastor asked me, "So, what exactly are we praying for?"

When the questions began to come, I realized that there were many people who, like me, were interested in night and day prayer but didn't know what the Bible said about it. The purpose of this book is to offer a biblical explanation of the prayer movement that is spreading across the earth. I pray that these pages provide you with clarity as you investigate God's agenda for prayer at the end of the age.

We live in an hour when many in the Church are groping for identity and direction. At the same time, God is revealing His purposes to His Bride so that she might partner with Him in His plans through prayer. According to Revelation 22:17, there is no doubt that the Church is ultimately destined to become a Praying Church at the end of the age. As you read, consider your calling to partner with the Lord in prayer unto seeing His plans come to pass in the earth.

MY JOURNEY INTO
INTERCESSION

A ching. Thirsting. Longing. No matter what word is used, it seems impossible to express the volcano of raging desire in a heart that has been branded by a true move of God's Spirit.

When I speak with those who have experienced a genuine visitation, all have the same response: "Once you taste it, nothing else will satisfy." There are many opinions about the nature of revival, but those who have been touched by it understand its nearly addicting effect. When God takes the field, flesh wilts under the relentless onslaught of His power. An insatiable desire is birthed in your heart as you encounter what you have been created for: God—unveiled and unrestrained.

I understand this ache, this gnawing, firsthand. As a young believer, I was fascinated by stories of historic revivals. My faith would soar as I listened to accounts of mass salvations, signs, wonders, and miracles. What began as an avid interest ripened into an aggressive pursuit of a massive outbreak of His Spirit.

Prayer for revival became my companion as my craving for God intensified. I had been in full-time ministry for several years and had enjoyed encounters with God's power before, yet a question still plagued me: "When will You move in our midst with revival?"

At that time, I was a youth pastor at a growing local church in a suburb just north of Atlanta. Our congregation had grown exponentially over the previous nine years as we had experienced God's great favor. Yet the outbreak of God for which my soul longed continued to elude us.

I realized there was a monumental difference between God blessing a church service with His presence and God moving on people with dramatic displays of His power and glory. The two are as different as water from a faucet is from a torrential downpour.

For years I had pursued God through prayer and fasting. Suddenly, in the fall of 2001, He came down upon our youth ministry. This move of His Spirit would forever mark my life. For about nine months, the manifest presence of God engulfed us. Like a thick cloud blanketing us with glory, God's power was manifest in every meeting. The fire of His love burned in our hearts as our longing for Him continued to increase; the more we received, the more we desired.

His power was portrayed through healings, signs, and wonders. We saw many testimonies of God's grace. A woman who had eczema for years walked through the room one night—she didn't stay for more than a few minutes—and, upon leaving, she examined her hands and found the eczema was completely gone! A young man who had suffered with a debilitating heart murmur his entire life was instantly healed; he was set free to run, jump, and praise God, which was something he could not do before. Countless times I witnessed God's presence overcoming people, crumpling them to the ground as His Spirit coursed through their being. Over 600 people made new commitments to Christ in a six-month period of time as the conviction of the Holy Spirit broke our hearts, leading many to repentance. I understood what Charles Finney described when he said, "If I had a sword in each hand, I could not have cut them off their seats as fast as they fell."[1]

It's still painful to admit, but just as suddenly as this visitation came, it dissipated. God continued to do good things in our midst—we still saw healings and conversions; however, the flame of His fire was no longer burning as strongly in our midst as before. His Spirit was still with us, for He never leaves us. Yet it was clear that the Divine Personality was no longer tangibly manifest among us.

Marked by Fire

I once heard a recording of a man who lived through an incredible revival in Scotland. With pain in his voice, he urged his listeners, "When you find it, *don't let it go!*" I now understood the ache in this man's plea. When the spirit of revival lifted, I found myself hungrier than ever. I had touched heaven, if just for a moment, and now that which I had pursued through years of prayer had departed. I felt the pain of longing rippling from my soul. I was comfortless—captive to my cravings. David spoke of this ache when he said, "As the deer pants, my soul longs for God" (Ps. 42:1). Do you know what it means to be ruined, completely reduced to desire?

I began to spend long hours in prayer, on my face before the Lord, trying to soothe the ache in my soul. I canceled appointments and rescheduled meetings, retreating

---

[1] Finney, Charles G., *Memoirs of Charles G. Finney* (New York: Fleming H. Revell Co., 1876), 103.

to the single place I found satisfaction—His presence. Hours passed instantly as I poured myself out before God.

For several months I attempted to gather myself in the wake of this bittersweet season. All I had sought in God had seemed to slip through my grasp. And now what was left? Church as usual? I could not go back to nice services, tidy testimonies, and plain proclamations. God had broken the box we had conveniently kept Him in, and I could no longer live with safe Christianity.

Now, I was in the wilderness of wanting without an exit. He bankrupted me to shatter all of my selfish ambitions. Popularity, platform, and persona lost their allure. What could possibly soothe the violent craving that was ransacking my heart? Only another deluge of His Spirit would suffice. But what I craved most was seemingly lost. What was I to do?

I had been so fervent in my desire for revival that in some ways I felt like the proverbial boy who cried wolf. In my heart, I knew there was more of God available than what I was experiencing. At first, many of my peers were encouraged and exhorted by my incessant passion for a move of the Spirit. However, over time, I became an irritant—unwilling to settle for "normal" Christianity. I found that those who passionately pursue more of God run the risk of unintentionally offending those who are satisfied with Christianity as is. I found myself aching and alone. Yet this season was divinely ordered and essential to bringing me into God's destiny for my life.

A New Vision

The Lord began to deal with me about contending for breakthrough, not just for my ministry, but instead for an entire city. He spoke to me about building a "beachhead in the Spirit" with concentrated intercession to shift the spiritual climate of the entire region. The vision in my heart for revival was no longer confined solely to my ministry. It was enlarged, encompassing the southeast, the US, and the nations of the earth. God was calling me into night and day prayer to be part of a historic outbreak of revival that would send shockwaves throughout the earth.

I had heard of the International House of Prayer in Kansas City some years earlier but knew very little about the ministry. I had read that Mike Bickle had started a twenty-four-hour prayer center, but, honestly, I thought it was a senseless waste of time. When I first heard of night and day prayer, I could not understand why someone would want to pray all day. But through that season of revival the Lord had broken me and prayer had become my only respite. It was clear that God was now calling me into something similar. How He loves to draw us into the very thing we disdain.

Through a series of prophetic events, God revealed to me that I was to move to Kansas City to learn the message and model of the house of prayer, in order to build a twenty-four-hour worship and prayer ministry in the city of Atlanta. I had now come to believe that ceaseless worship and intercession would be a key to opening the gates in our city, unleashing an awakening of epic proportions.

As I embarked upon this vision, God began to open the Scriptures to me in a way I had not experienced before. He diminished me and enlarged Himself. My understanding of His plan was dramatically amplified. Now, nearly a decade later, I am beginning to understand that God released that season of revival in order to engage me

in a much broader kingdom agenda. The season of revival was only an appetizer to prepare me for God's main
course. He planted a seed in my soul that continues to
grow to this day.

While revival remains a relentless pursuit of my heart
and my longings for God persist, I now realize that God
used my passion for revival to position me in the global
tapestry of worship and intercession He is weaving together throughout the nations. God is raising up an end-
time prayer movement that will culminate in massive
revival, end-time judgments, and the return of the Lord
Jesus to rule and reign on the earth. Through the rollercoaster ride of God's visitation and its subsequent reces-
sion, the only thing that comforted and stabilized my soul
was prayer. Ultimately, the pursuit of revival drew me into
the ministry of intercession.

The Journey into Intercession

Now, still searching for another move of God, I find
myself leading a community whose intercessory cry has
echoed through heaven's halls continuously since 2006.
The perfection of God's plan is astounding. Years ago, as
a youth pastor, God instilled in me with an unquenchable
passion for revival. Never would I have dreamt that God,
through this pursuit, would propel me into the middle
of the very movement that will precipitate the return of
His Son (see the chapters "Night and Day Prayer in the
Earth Today" and "Speedy Justice"). So, rather than solely
believing for a regional revival, I've set my face toward a
higher vision. I am contending for the Church's global
end-time awakening to prayer, which will hasten the day
of the Lord's return. God has reserved the greatest move

of His Spirit for a future day, and you and I are invited to partner with Him through prayer to welcome it to the earth.

Possibly you are like me, and the cry for "more" resounds in the deepest part of your being. Maybe you have experienced seasons of visitation that have left you longing for something lasting. Or perhaps you have recently been stirred to seek God in prayer in a greater measure than you have ever known. It could be that the rising tide of night and day prayer in the earth has piqued your interest, drawing you to investigate what's written in the pages of this book. Whatever the case, each of us has a unique experience that has brought us to this most incredible moment. We are at the onset of a global tidal wave of prayer that will culminate with the Lord Jesus' return to the planet. We are peering over a precipice to the greatest hour in human history. Could it be that you are part of a generation that God is raising up, who, like Esther, is appointed for such a time as this to entreat the favor of the King?

In this book we will journey together to investigate the prophetic, historic, and biblical foundations of the current prayer movement that is sweeping the globe. It could be that you, like me, are destined to pursue God in prayer "until"—until His presence once again possesses His people, until "good" prayer meetings give way to glory, until masses of lost souls find salvation, until revival breaks across the nations like floodwaters shattering a dam, until He judges the earth and avenges His Bride, and until He returns and takes the nations as His possession. Let us consider together the prayer movement that God is initiating in this hour and His ultimate agenda to conclude this age. My prayer is that you will be gripped with a vision for intercession and that you will cry out in prayer night and day until He comes.

THE ORIGIN OF THE TABERNACLE OF DAVID

> So Samuel did what the LORD said, and went to Bethlehem. And the elders of the town trembled at his coming, and said, "Do you come peaceably?"
> —1 Samuel 16:4

Imagine the day that Samuel, the Lord's prophet, approached the meager village of Bethlehem. Bethlehem was one of the least important cities of Judah, and now the greatest prophet Israel had ever known was approaching.

Samuel was incredibly powerful. He had never given a prophecy that did not come to pass (1 Sam. 3:19). His reputation was renowned throughout the entire nation. Once, as he proclaimed the word of the Lord, God released supernatural thunder upon the Philistines, throwing them into confusion and fear, and ultimately bringing about their defeat. Because of Samuel's powerful prophetic ministry, the Philistines were driven away from the towns of Israel throughout the entirety of his life (1 Sam. 7:13).

Undoubtedly his purpose in coming to tiny Bethlehem was to deliver a prophetic oracle that would have great impact upon the people. His very presence was fearsome. No wonder the town elders trembled at his coming!

Instead of making a great proclamation throughout the city, Samuel visited a simple townsman named Jesse. There is no record that Samuel had any previous dealings with Jesse, who must have been astonished—this powerful prophet had come to his town, called him by name, and gathered the town elders together to attend a sacrifice in his home! What could this mean?

Samuel told Jesse to summon his sons, so Jesse brought each one before the great prophet. But after seven sons had passed before Samuel's eyes, Samuel knew by the Spirit of the Lord that one was still missing.

"Are these all the sons you have?" Samuel asked.

"There is still the youngest, but he is tending the sheep," Jesse said with a hint of embarrassment.

"We will not sit down until he arrives," Samuel replied, convinced that this one would be the Lord's choice.

How could the young, red-haired shepherd boy who had been disregarded by his father comprehend what was about to happen? He was from the least significant town of his tribe, Judah, and he was the least within his family. Yet, the days and nights he spent faithfully serving his father's house, worshiping with his harp while watching over the sheep, had qualified him to be God's choice to shepherd His people, Israel. When David was called to the gathering, imagine his shock when Samuel stepped forward and poured the horn of oil over him, anointing him in the name of the Lord as king of Israel!

Promotion and Demotion

And David behaved wisely in all his ways, and the LORD was with him.

—1 Samuel 18:14

David's life was turned upside down from that moment forward. He was supernaturally empowered in all that he did. As a teen defending his father's sheep, he easily killed a lion and a bear with his bare hands. He was an anointed musician, who, with a song, could drive demons from those who were tormented.

When he was a young man, God anointed him to defeat Goliath, the mightiest warrior of the Philistines. As a result, when he was nearly twenty years old, Saul appointed him as captain over the entire military force of Israel. The entire nation rallied around him. Even the young women wrote songs about his great exploits. What an amazing turn of events! God took David from guarding sheep in the forgotten city of Bethlehem to commanding all the forces of Israel, leading the nation in powerful military victories.

This was not the only dramatic turnaround that young David would experience. As quickly as he grew in popularity with the people, he became an object of scorn and hatred to Saul. The anointing and favor of God upon David's life infuriated Saul. Saul recognized God's favor upon David and feared that David would replace him as king. David's greatest ally morphed into his greatest enemy almost overnight. Seething with jealousy, Saul demoted David, removed him from his court and attempted to murder him. As a result, David fled for his life and Saul issued a command to all of his servants that if any found David, they should kill him.

David Flees to Ramah

> So David fled and escaped, and went to Samuel at Ramah, and told him all that Saul had done to him.

And he and Samuel went and stayed in Naioth.
                                    —1 Samuel 19:18

Rather than being the valiant commander of Israel's
army, David was now a fugitive whom the army commanders were seeking to assassinate. David had experienced a rollercoaster ride of success and rejection. He
was completely alienated from the men he once led. And
worse, the man he considered to be a spiritual father now
sought his life. In the face of these troubling and painful
circumstances, David turned to the man who was respon-
sible for initiating these events—Samuel.

For many years Samuel had lived in his hometown
of Ramah, where he developed a school of the prophets,
discipling young men with prophetic giftings in worship,
prayer, and prophecy. When David arrived in Ramah, he
told Samuel all that had transpired between him and Saul.

Within a short time, Saul sent assassins to Ramah
to murder David. Though the men had come to murder
David, when they arrived, the Spirit of the Lord divinely
intercepted them. As they approached the company of
prophets, the power of God came upon them and they began to prophesy the word of the Lord. Upon returning to
Saul, they explained to him why they had not completed
their assignment.

Saul sent two more groups of assassins to execute David. Each time, the Spirit of the Lord intercepted them,
causing them to prophesy. It is likely that Saul was curi-
ous about these prophecies and inquired of his men what
it was that God caused them to proclaim. Perhaps they
prophesied the very thing that Samuel had prophesied
over David years earlier in Bethlehem: "David will be
king and ascend to the throne of Israel." Imagine how

that must have troubled Saul!

Determined to destroy David, Saul took matters into his own hands. He traveled to Ramah, but just as with his assassins, the Spirit of the Lord broke in upon him and he prophesied all night under the influence of the Spirit of God. Perhaps Saul prophesied David's kingship too.

Unprecedented spiritual activity was taking place in Ramah. What was so important to God that He would pour out His Spirit upon executioners and transform them into oracles? What was the Lord emphasizing through this powerful manifestation of His Spirit?

David's time spent with the prophet Samuel must have been extremely significant. Ramah was approximately twenty miles from Gibeah, where Saul was stationed. It would have taken several weeks for Saul to learn of David's presence in Ramah, send three envoys of assassins, and finally travel there himself. So David must have remained in Ramah for several weeks.

What did David and Samuel talk about while he was there? It was something so essential, so monumental to the kingdom of God, that God saw to it that no man's wicked plan could thwart His purposes. 1 Chronicles 9:22 gives us the details of this vitally important meeting.

Blueprints for the Tabernacle

> All those chosen as gatekeepers were two hundred and twelve. They were recorded by their genealogy, in their villages. David and Samuel the seer had appointed them to their trusted office.
> —1 Chronicles 9:22

The tabernacle of David was a tent that housed a night and day worship and prayer meeting before the ark of the

Lord. Samuel and David initially formulated the plans and strategy for the first house of prayer. But Samuel died many years before the tabernacle was actually built (1 Sam. 25:1). When, then, did Samuel and David conceive of the plan for the tabernacle? I believe it was while David was in Ramah. Other than that time and David's anointing in Bethlehem, there is no other biblical account of David and Samuel spending time together. So the plans for the tabernacle of David were likely drawn up while David was in Ramah. When God thwarted Saul and his assassins, He was protecting His plans for night and day prayer as the centerpiece of His kingdom on earth.

Though David had fled to Ramah, hoping Samuel would get him out of trouble with Saul, God had had quite a different plan. Perhaps David's dialogue with Samuel went something like this:

"Samuel, what did you do to me? After you anointed me, everything in my life changed. For a little while, things were great. I was stronger than ever. I killed a lion, a bear, and great warriors with ease. I was promoted into the military and became head of the armed forces. On top of that, my singing and playing improved; I was anointed for worship like never before. Demons fled when I played my harp. It was incredible—until Saul decided I was his enemy. What do I do now? I am a fugitive and Saul's assassins are after me. They've probably tracked me to Ramah and are coming to murder me. Please, do something! You're a prophet. Help!"

The aged prophet may have replied, "David, my son, do you think God, who chose you out of the sheepfold, would let you die at the hands of Saul? You have no idea who you are. Listen to me very carefully. Much more is going on than you know. God has anointed you to make you a living prophecy of Messiah who is to come.[1] That's right, young man, your entire life is going to be a prophetic picture that will point people to God's Son, who will one day rule the earth. The Lord has spoken to me very clearly about a plan that He wants you to carry out. He desires night and day worship before the ark, and He wants you to set it up. It will mirror the worship around the throne in heaven. Just as His throne is the centerpiece of all authority and dominion, when you set up ceaseless worship on the earth, great dominion will be given to you in your kingdom. When you were on the backside of the desert watching over those sheep and worshiping the Lord, the Lord told me that you were a man after His own heart—one who would do His will. This is your destiny. This is who you are!"

Can you imagine David's shock when he first heard that he would be a prophetic picture of the Messiah to come? The Lord gave David several weeks with Samuel at Ramah, in the school of the prophets, to help David comprehend God's destiny for his life. When the assassins and Saul himself showed up to kill David and instead began to prophesy, Samuel's words to David about his destiny and the tabernacle of worship were confirmed.

God divinely appointed David's time in Ramah, not only to impart His strategy for the tabernacle, but also to strengthen him. David would spend the next seven years of his life fleeing Saul's fury, so the Lord used this strategic meeting to impress upon David's heart the importance of his destiny. In future years, when David would be forced to live in caves and foreign cities, he would need to draw upon this prophetic encounter for courage in order

[1]   Isa. 55:3–4.

to persevere and accomplish all that God had planned.

David would not gain his throne until he was thirty years old, after both Saul and his heir had died. Once David ascended to the throne of Israel, the first thing he did was retake Jerusalem from the Jebusites, who had fortified themselves on top of Mount Zion. Once he conquered and removed the Jebusites, he retrieved the ark of God and brought it to Jerusalem. In obedience to the Lord's plan, he set up night and day worship as the central facet of his kingdom, and Israel prospered greatly. From that time forward, night and day prayer became the blueprint for corporate worship for the people of God throughout Israel's successive generations. In the next chapter, we will investigate the biblical accounts of night and day prayer, from Moses to David and beyond.

BIBLICAL ACCOUNTS OF
NIGHT AND DAY PRAYER

In the days of the exodus, about 1,000 years before David's tabernacle was built, God directed Moses to build a tabernacle in the wilderness so that His people could worship Him. He gave Moses very specific instructions regarding the construction of the tabernacle, as well as the regulations for the order of worship. The writer of Hebrews tells us that this tabernacle and its order of worship were symbolic of the heavenly worship that takes place before the throne of God, and of the eternal sacrifice that Christ offered in His own blood for the redemption of all mankind (Heb. 9:1–12).

One of the most interesting features of Moses' tabernacle was the daily burnt offering that was offered to the Lord every morning and every evening (Ex. 29:38–42). The burnt offering was to be a one-year-old lamb without spot or blemish, and was to be sacrificed by the priest and offered upon the altar. The fire upon the altar was never to go out (Lev. 6:13), aflame all day and all night. God wanted it to stay lit to signify a continual reality of worship and devotion from God's people toward Himself.

The first account we have of the high priest offering

the daily burnt offering is found in Leviticus 9. After Aaron had been consecrated to the Lord and set apart to his priestly office, he was to offer a burnt offering to the Lord. Once he offered the burnt offering and several other offerings, he and Moses blessed the people. After this, the glory of the Lord appeared to the whole congregation. Fire shot out from the presence of the Lord and consumed the burnt offering.

Can you imagine the sight of the glory of God appearing in plain view to over two million people? The flash of God's fire was so powerful that all the people shouted and fell on their faces. The altar was set ablaze with heavenly glory (Lev. 9:23–24). It was this consuming fire that burned night and day upon the altar throughout Israel's sojourn in the wilderness. The priests fueled it every morning and every night with fresh wood, removing the ashes from the previous sacrifice and offering another lamb (Lev. 6:12–13).

This fire was symbolic of the continual devotion that God desires from His people. God was the One who supplied the heavenly fire, but it was the priests' responsibility to make sure it kept burning by continuing to offer sacrifices and by putting wood on the fire. The offering was a sweet aroma to the Lord (Ex. 29:41). In this same manner, the Lord ignites our hearts with His holy fire. And like the priests of old, it is our responsibility to make sure that we continually offer our hearts to Him in worship and adoration to keep the fire burning brightly within us.

Tabernacle of David, 1050 BC

> So he left Asaph and his relatives there before the
> ark of the covenant of the LORD to minister before

the ark continually, as every day's work required.

—1 Chronicles 16:37, NASB

It was David who first understood that the Lord longed for hearts who would continually offer worship and praise to God. He understood that worship and praise from a sincere heart would bless the Lord more than burnt offerings (Ps. 69:30–31). David's heart of love and devotion to the Lord caused him to establish a new order of worship in Israel.

In approximately 1050 BC, David set up a tent in Jerusalem where night and day worship with singers and musicians took place before the ark of God. This tent was called the tabernacle of David. This reality of worship was *in addition* to the offerings that were already being offered to the Lord in the tabernacle of Moses at Gibeon. The two realities of worship continued to operate simultaneously throughout the entirety of David's reign. David kept both forms of worship operating because he understood that one was symbolic of the other—the fire that burned perpetually on the altar in the tabernacle of Moses was a symbol of the night and day worship taking place in the tabernacle of David.

God longed to be continually intimate with His people. He wanted to engage with His people twenty-four hours a day. He wanted the hearts of His people to continually burn with His very own passion and fire. Thus, David's tabernacle continued in ceaseless worship and adoration to the Lord as an answer to God's desire for continual intimacy with His people.

Worship in David's tabernacle took place before the ark of the Lord in an open forum where male and female, Jew and proselyte (Gentile converts to Judaism) could come and worship freely.

The tabernacle of David used 288 Levites who were gifted in singing the prophetic songs of the Lord (1 Chr. 25:7). These singers were broken down into twenty-four teams, each with twelve members (1 Chr. 25:9–31). This group of gifted singers led a larger group of 4,000 musicians. They used instruments that David designed himself (1 Chr. 23:5). Another 4,000 gatekeepers took care of the service of the tabernacle. Altogether, 8,000 Levites were employed full-time to offer night and day worship and praise before the ark of the Lord. In this environment, David wrote the majority of his psalms.

Immediately after David set up night and day prayer, the Lord gave him two amazing promises. He promised David that He would give him dominion by establishing his house forever. This meant that there would never cease to be a king from David's family line ruling upon the throne of Israel (2 Sam. 7:8–16). The second promise was even more astounding. God promised David that the Messiah would come from this line of kings. In other words, Messiah would be a "son of David."

God gave these promises to David as a direct result of David's desire to establish night and day prayer. The promise of dominion that God gave to David was not only a reality throughout David's life, but was also a reality for every king of Judah who established night and day prayer under his own leadership.

Six other kings of Judah practiced night and day prayer according to the Davidic model. Each of these kings experienced seasons of blessing and revival in his kingdom. When a king did not keep the Davidic order of worship, the kingdom would begin to lose direction and the people would give themselves to idol worship.

Solomon, 1010 BC

And, according to the order of David his father, he appointed the divisions of the priests for their service . . . for so David the man of God had commanded.

—2 Chronicles 8:14

In approximately 1010 BC, Solomon, David's son, completed the temple of the Lord. Solomon commanded that the temple worship should be in accordance with the Davidic order (2 Chr. 8:14–15). In the temple, Solomon combined the night and day worship from the tabernacle of David with the sacrificial system from the tabernacle of Moses. At the dedication of the temple, the glory of the Lord appeared with such power that the priests could not stand to minister (2 Chr. 5:14). The powerful manifestation of God's presence testified of the Lord's approval of the temple, the ministry of night and day worship, and His pleasure with His people.

During Solomon's reign, there was an open heaven over Israel, and God's presence and blessing were continually manifest among the people. The Lord appeared to Solomon on two different occasions. On the first occasion, the Lord said to Solomon, "Ask! What shall I give you?" Solomon asked for wisdom, and the Lord endowed Him with more wisdom than anyone who had ever lived. With his God-given understanding, Solomon made decisions that caused the kingdom of Israel to multiply in greatness. The people were so financially prosperous that silver was considered common and not even valuable during Solomon's reign (1 Kgs. 10:21).

The dominion that the Lord promised David was manifest during the reign of Solomon. God exalted Israel in an unprecedented way and the nation experienced unprecedented peace and prosperity. Unfortunately, this prosperity and blessing did not last. In Solomon's later years, he turned away from the Lord and began to worship the gods of his foreign wives. Because of this tragic mistake, the kingdom became divided and went into years of backsliding and idol worship.

Joash and Jehoiada, 853 BC

> And they offered burnt offerings in the house of the LORD continually all the days of Jehoiada.
> —2 Chronicles 24:14

After the reign of Solomon, the kingdom became divided. Ten of the tribes of Israel split and moved to the north, making their capital Samaria, while two tribes remained in the south, with their capital in Jerusalem. The northern kingdom never served the Lord. The south went through seasons of backsliding and revival, depending upon the leadership of the current king.

Approximately 125 years after Solomon, Jehoshaphat, a righteous king, ascended to the throne of the southern kingdom. However, the years following his reign were dark times for the kingdom of Judah. Though Jehoshaphat had served the Lord with all his heart, he made a fatal political error. In an effort to bring peace between the northern and southern kingdoms, he agreed to marry Athaliah, the daughter of Ahab and Jezebel—the wicked monarchs of the north. Ahab and Jezebel had led the entire nation of Israel to worship Baal, and their daughter was no different.

After Jehoshaphat died, his son Ahaziah ruled Judah. His reign was cut short by Jehu, who had been anointed to destroy all from the household of Ahab (2 Kgs. 9:6–8).

When Jehu killed Ahaziah only one year into Ahaziah's reign, his mother Athaliah seized the throne. Her lust for power and her wicked ambition drove her to kill all of her grandsons. She wanted to blot out the royal seed so that she could rule Judah as queen.

Her plan succeeded, except in one point. Her daughter, Jehosheba, hid Joash, Athaliah's grandson, in the temple of the Lord under the care of the priest Jehoiada. For six years Athaliah reigned in Judah, spreading her wickedness and Baal worship throughout the kingdom. But when Joash was seven years old, Jehoiada made a covenant with the military commanders to restore Joash, the rightful heir, to the throne. The commanders of the military killed Athaliah, and Joash, the rightful heir from the line of David, became king in her place. The people rejoiced and the city was at peace, having been delivered from Athaliah's wicked ways (2 Kgs. 11).

Joash cleansed and restored the temple. He reinstituted the practice of giving offerings to the priests to provide for their living expenses. Athaliah's sons had desecrated the temple of the Lord, so Joash commanded that the offerings he collected be used to restore the temple and reinstate the priesthood. Joash, under the guidance of Jehoiada the priest, also reinstated the temple service with the daily burnt offerings and the Davidic order of night and day worship. Under his leadership the people of Judah tore down the temple of Baal and killed its priest. The nation experienced a season of revival as the people turned away from Baal worship and gave themselves in abandonment to the Lord (2 Kgs. 11–12). The restoration of the daily offerings and night and day worship led to this season of renewal in Judah.

Hezekiah, 726 BC

> He stationed the Levites in the house of the LORD
> with cymbals, with stringed instruments, and with
> harps, according to the commandment of David.
>   —2 Chronicles 29:25

Hezekiah ruled in Judah 125 years after Joash. He was
the son of Ahaz. Ahaz had been a very wicked king who
had encouraged moral decline in Judah and been rebel-
lious toward the Lord. He offered sacrifices to the gods
of the nations that had defeated him in battle, and he
discontinued the worship of the Lord in the temple. He
actually shut up the doors of the temple so that no one
could enter. He took the holy articles from the temple and
cut them into pieces. He set up altars to false gods in every
town of Judah and provoked the Lord to anger. Because
of him, the Lord allowed Judah to be conquered by Syria
(2 Chr. 28:5).

When Hezekiah became king, he realized Judah and
Jerusalem's problems were due to their abandonment of
the Lord and their worship of false gods. So he set out to
reform the kingdom. As soon as he took the throne, he reopened the temple and had the priests work to restore everything that had been destroyed. He again employed the
Levites in offering the daily sacrifices and in practicing
night and day worship, according to the order of David.
He called the *entire* nation of Israel, from the northern
and southern kingdoms of Israel and Judah, to come and
celebrate the Passover feast. The people returned to the
Lord under his leadership, and Judah prospered greatly.
The nation had not experienced the blessing of the Lord
in this manner since the days of Solomon.

During the reign of Hezekiah, the king of Assyria

attempted to besiege Jerusalem and take the people captive. Twenty years earlier, Assyria had invaded and destroyed the northern kingdom of Israel. Now the southern kingdom was under siege. The Lord told Hezekiah to resist the Assyrian king and to cry out to the Lord for deliverance. In one night, the angel of the Lord destroyed 185,000 soldiers from the Assyrian army, bringing a stunning victory and deliverance to Hezekiah and the people of Judah (2 Chr. 32). Perhaps only when the Lord delivered Israel from Egypt had Israel ever experienced such a supernatural deliverance from her enemies.

When Hezekiah reopened the temple, reinstituted the daily sacrifices, and reestablished the Davidic order of worship, the Lord began to bless the nation in an incredible way. National repentance and revival broke out among the people. The Lord caused the nation to turn back to Him. He greatly prospered them and once again gave them dominion—just as He had promised David. As long as night and day prayer was the centerpiece of the nation, God brought great blessing, power, and deliverance to His people.

Josiah, 635 BC

> The singers, the sons of Asaph, were in their places, according to the command of David.
> —2 Chronicles 35:15

After Hezekiah died, his son Manasseh ruled for fifty-five years in Judah. Manasseh did not follow the ways of the Lord, but instead led the people into extreme wickedness. He rebuilt the altars to the false gods that his father had destroyed, and he set up idols in the house of the Lord.

Later in his life, Manasseh humbled himself before God and turned back to the Lord, but the nation had gone terribly astray. His son Amon ruled after him and committed the same sins that he had. When Amon was murdered, his son Josiah took the throne.

Josiah was eight years old when he became king in Jerusalem. He aggressively pursued the Lord at the age of sixteen, and by the time he was twenty years old, he began tearing down all the altars to false gods that had been set up throughout Judah. Soon, he had thoroughly purged the land by destroying all the high places and altars used to worship false gods.

During his reign, the priests found the book of the Law of Moses that had been lost and read it to Josiah. When he heard the words of the Lord, he knew that the nation was in danger of judgment, for the people had departed from the ways of the Lord. Josiah wept and repented on behalf of the people. The Lord answered him and told him that though judgment was indeed coming, God was going to give the people a season of clemency. He reassured Josiah that as long as he was alive, the Lord would not release the appointed judgment upon the people (2 Chr. 34:23–28).

Josiah reestablished the Passover, as his great-grandfather Hezekiah had done. He also reinstituted the Davidic order of worship in the service of the temple (2 Chr. 35:3-4). Josiah's reforms brought about a season of revival and the release of the mercy of the Lord to Judah. When the people turned to the Lord, and while the Levites practiced night and day worship, the nation continued to prosper

Zerubbabel, 538 BC

When the builders laid the foundation of the temple of the LORD, the priests stood in their apparel with trumpets, and the Levites, the sons of Asaph, with cymbals, to praise the LORD, according to the ordinance of David king of Israel.

—Ezra 3:10

In 606 BC, the Babylonian army swept down upon Jerusalem, destroying the temple, burning the city, and taking the remnant of Israel captive. God allowed this to happen because His people had once again turned away from Him and disregarded His ordinances. God raised up the nation of Babylon as an instrument of His judgment but prophesied through Jeremiah that after seventy years, the people would be released from their captivity and would return to Jerusalem (Jer. 25:11–12, 29:10).

After sixty-nine years of captivity, Daniel, having understood the prophecies of Jeremiah, cried out to the Lord to keep His word and deliver God's people from captivity. God was true to His promise. In 536 BC, exactly seventy years after the Babylonian invasion, He stirred up the heart of the Persian king, Cyrus, to release the Jewish captives so that they could return to Jerusalem and rebuild the temple of the Lord (Ezra 1:1–2). Cyrus commissioned all who desired to return, to complete the task of rebuilding the temple.

Approximately fifty thousand Jews returned to Jerusalem, traveling hundreds of miles across the desert on foot to rebuild the house of the Lord. Once the foundation was laid, the singers and Levites were commissioned to reestablish night and day worship according to the order of David.

They understood that the desire of the Lord was for

more than just a building, but that it was for a people who would pursue a continuous reality of worship and adoration of His name. It would be another twenty years until the temple was completed. As long as the people practiced night and day worship, they prospered; but when they lost their focus, they faltered. Clearly, night and day worship and prayer was the Lord's central purpose in bringing His people out of captivity.

Nehemiah, 446 BC

> Both the singers and the gatekeepers kept the charge of their God and the charge of the purification, according to the command of David and Solomon his son. For in the days of David and Asaph of old there were chiefs of the singers, and songs of praise and thanksgiving to God. In the days of Zerubbabel and in the days of Nehemiah all Israel gave the portions for the singers and the gatekeepers, a portion for each day. They also consecrated holy things for the Levites, and the Levites consecrated them for the children of Aaron.
> —Nehemiah 12:45–47

About seventy years after the temple was rebuilt, the Lord stirred Nehemiah, a Jew still living in Babylon, to move to his homeland and oversee the rebuilding of the wall surrounding Jerusalem. He had heard that Jerusalem was in great distress and that the wall had been broken down (Neh. 1:3). Nehemiah was a trusted servant and the cupbearer to Artaxerxes, the king of Persia. When he explained to the king that his heart was deeply grieved because of the condition of his people and his nation, the king granted his request, allowing him to go to Jerusalem to assess the state of his people and to offer aid.

When Nehemiah arrived, what he beheld justified the burden upon his heart. The people were greatly disheartened and the wall was still in ruins, having been burned to the ground some ninety years earlier. The city was without protection from neighboring nations. Were it not for the protection of Persia, marauding raiders would once again have ransacked Jerusalem.

Upon Nehemiah's arrival, he quickly rallied some of the leaders and put together a plan to rebuild the wall around the city. The neighboring nations had been extremely hostile toward the Jews and did not want to see them prosper. Amidst much opposition from the other nations, Nehemiah led the Jews in rebuilding the wall in only fifty-two days (Neh. 6:15).

Though the temple had been rebuilt in the time of Zerubbabel, the Jews had been negligent in providing for the Levites so that they could be employed in the service of the house of the Lord in night and day prayer. This troubled Nehemiah greatly. Immediately after the wall was completed, Nehemiah, filled with the zeal of the Lord, appointed gatekeepers, singers, and Levites to reinstitute the practice of night and day worship (Neh. 7:1). He made sure that the nation continued to provide for the Levites so that night and day prayer continued during his lifetime (Neh. 12–13).

My House Shall Be Called a House of Prayer

> And He said to them, "It is written, 'My house shall be called a house of prayer,' but you have made it a 'den of thieves.'"
>
> —Matthew 21:13

When Jesus showed up in the very same temple nearly
five hundred years after Nehemiah, it was evident that He
was greatly disturbed that moneychangers were buying
and selling in the temple courts. They were greedily prof-
iting by selling the necessary wares for worship on the
Passover. The powerful rebuke that He levied against the
people made evident the principle issue upon his heart—
He burned with desire for the night and day reality of
prayer, which had become nothing more than a distant
memory to the people.

The priests had accommodated those who were greedy
for gain, allowing them to practice their "trade" in the
courts of the Lord. At the same time, they neglected the
intimacy of true worship and prayer that the Lord so desired. Even though daily sacrifices continued to be offered
in the temple, the practice had become a mere ritual, lack-
ing any true intimacy between the people and God.

Jesus had walked into these very temple courts three
years earlier and had driven out the moneychangers with
a whip (Jn. 2:15–16). Here, near the end of His life, He
once again zealously confronted those who were commer-
cially capitalizing on the feast of Passover. Nowhere else
in the gospels did Jesus physically engage with people to
obstruct them from their sin.

Jesus initiated and finalized His ministry by cleansing
the temple. These two acts are bookends of His earthly
ministry. What compelled Him to accentuate His ministry in this way? His piercing proclamation, "My house
shall be called a house of prayer," vividly identifies the basis for his fervor. When Jesus made this declaration, it
was as if He was saying, "Where is the prayer? You know
that My Father has always dreamed of continual worship
and intimacy with His people. How could you replace the

very thing my Father's heart longs for with commerce and greed?"

His words fell on deaf ears. Only a few days later, the nation of Israel would crucify her king, putting Him to death in the same way common criminals were executed. Within forty years, Jerusalem would be besieged and destroyed by the Roman army. They had exchanged their devotion to God for financial gain and religious ritual—all to their demise.

Could it be in the Church today that we too have exchanged simple intimacy for prosperity and performance? Perhaps we have become mired in the same pitfalls that seduced first-century Israel. We must remember that rather than bringing financial prosperity, Israel's departure from intimacy with God and negligence regarding night and day prayer resulted in their ultimate destruction.

It is evident throughout Scripture that when God's people practiced night and day worship and prayer, the nation prospered and God released revival and blessing upon them. But when they neglected continual devotion to the Lord, they were led astray and worshiped idols, hence bringing God's disfavor upon themselves.

Night and day prayer was not something the Lord called David alone to practice. Rather, it was to be the centerpiece of the corporate worship experience for God's people throughout every generation. Since the Scriptures so establish fully God's desire for night and day worship, why should we think that the Lord desires anything less from believers today?

God wants to release kingdom authority and dominion through His people in this hour, just as He released it through David. As in David's reign, when the authority of the kingdom was manifest in the earth as a result of night and day prayer, God is raising up twenty-four-hour prayer unto the release of that same authority and government. As God establishes night and day prayer throughout the earth in this generation, we are truly going to see the prayer of Jesus answered: "Thy Kingdom come, thy will be done, in earth as it is in heaven" (Mt. 6:10, KJV).

Malachi's Prophecy

The worship that took place in Solomon's temple combined two key elements: the daily sacrifices that the Lord had prescribed to Moses, and the ceaseless worship practiced in the tabernacle of David. As we have already discussed, when the nation of Israel practiced night and day worship, they prospered greatly, but when they neglected it, they fell into sin.

After Israel's return from Babylonian exile, they went through yet another season of backsliding. Because of their contempt for continuous worship and prayer, God raised up the prophet Malachi to rebuke the wayward nation. Malachi described in detail a shift in God's plan for night and day worship. He said that a day would come when the temple would no longer be the only place of ceaseless worship—the Lord's praises would fill Gentile nations throughout the earth: "'From the rising of the sun, even to its going down, My name shall be great among the Gentiles; in every place incense shall be offered to My name, and a pure offering: for My name shall be great among the nations,' says the LORD of hosts" (Mal. 1:11). This was unthinkable to the Jews at that time. How could it be that Gentiles would engage in continuous adoration of Jehovah?

Malachi's prophecies proclaimed a transition from God's dwelling being solely among the nation of Israel to being among people from all nations. In essence, the Lord was saying through Malachi, "Because you have dealt treacherously with Me in regard to My desire for continuous worship and prayer, I am going to take it from you and give it to the Gentiles."

Jesus' Call for Night and Day Worship

As we discussed in the previous section, when Jesus came to the temple in the final week of His life, His zeal for the house of prayer burned so intensely that He overthrew the merchants' tables and expelled the moneychangers. With blazing passion, He quoted the prophet Isaiah, saying, "It is written, 'My house shall be called a house of prayer'" (Mt. 21:13).

It is important to note the context of Isaiah's prophecy so that we can fully understand Jesus' intentions in quoting this verse. Isaiah 56 speaks of a future time when God's salvation will be fully manifest and His righteousness completely revealed in the earth (Isa. 56:1). This will take place in the next age, when Jesus Himself will rule from Jerusalem. In that day, people from all nations will journey to Jerusalem to worship the Lord (Ps. 86:9; Isa. 2:2, 66:18; Hag. 2:7; Zech. 14:16). The ultimate fulfillment of the temple becoming a house of prayer for all nations is actually reserved for this future time. When the temple was still standing, only Jews were allowed to come into the temple courts—Gentiles were not admitted. In the age to come, however, worshipers from all nations will be drawn to Jerusalem and admitted into the temple to praise and glorify Jesus.

By quoting Isaiah's prophecy, Jesus was pointing ahead to this future time. He was proclaiming the far-reaching vision of God concerning His house of prayer. In doing so, He was tying God's future purpose into His plan for night and day prayer in this age. *The temple was always intended to function as an international house of prayer.* God never changed the corporate worship design for the people of God. He never revoked His command to Moses: "The fire on the altar shall be kept burning on it; it shall not be put out" (Lev. 6:12). The very centerpiece of kingdom culture and the corporate worship expression for God's people in the age to come will be night and day prayer. Could it be that Jesus was pointing to this future reality to express that continuous worship and prayer should be the standard for corporate worship in this age?

The Millennial Reality

Amos prophesied of a future day when the tabernacle of David would be rebuilt (Amos 9:11–15). Isaiah prophesied that Jesus would rule upon a throne in the rebuilt tabernacle of David (Isa. 16:5). Zechariah proclaimed that Jesus would be a priest, ruling from a throne in the temple (Zech. 6:12–13). All of these prophecies have yet to come to pass, but will one day be fulfilled when Jesus returns to rule the nations. Jesus will rule from the tabernacle of David with night and day worship and prayer taking place before His throne.

In heaven, worship choruses continue before the Father's throne incessantly. The living creatures and the twenty-four elders, along with the myriads of angels and saints, worship the Lord in perpetual perfection. The heavenly throne room is ablaze with beauty and sound.

It operates as an eternal night and day worship center (Rev. 4:8). When Jesus returns, He will set up His throne on the earth as a mirror of the Father's throne in heaven. Day and night prayer and worship will be offered to the Lord. Imagine that day when all nations will come and bow down in worship and adoration before the Lord Jesus Himself. This is our destiny and God's ultimate plan for the general worship assembly for His people in the coming ages.

The Common Thread

Night and day worship and prayer is a consistent thread weaving together the Old and New Testaments, as well as the age to come. Is it possible that we have overlooked this core facet of biblical corporate worship? The apostles were well aware of the essential nature of the tabernacle of David. In the Jerusalem council, they quoted Amos's prophecy speaking of the day the tabernacle would be rebuilt and serve as a light to the nations (Acts 15:16–17). They identified the standard of unity in worship in the tabernacle of David as essential for unity between Jewish and Gentile believers under the new covenant.

The fact that James, the leader of the gathering, chose to quote from the prophecy of Amos is significant. There are many Old Testament verses James could have referenced to illustrate the Gentiles' participation in the kingdom of God. However, he intentionally selected a verse that describes the reestablishment of the tabernacle of David. This implies that the apostles considered the vision for night and day prayer not only to be an Old Testament phenomenon, but also a New Testament reality.

Let's not forget that David, the greatest psalmist in

the Bible, wrote the majority of his psalms from the place of night and day worship and prayer. The throne room in heaven is a place of continuous worship and praise; shouldn't the community of faith resemble this heavenly pattern? Was there a time when the Lord instructed His people to stop worshiping Him night and day? Or is it possible that we, like the nation of Israel, have neglected the very thing that the Lord always desired—an incessant expression of worship from His beloved?

Some may argue that in the new covenant, believers *are* the temple of the Holy Spirit, that we no longer need a corporate expression of ceaseless worship. However, throughout the Bible, the Lord encourages His people to exercise night and day worship and prayer, and nowhere in Scripture do we see the Lord give the command for it to cease. Also, the corporate expression of worship has always been a symbol of the internal reality of the relationship we share with the Lord. Under the old covenant, temple worship was a prophetic picture of the abiding intimacy the Lord longed to have with His people, both corporately and individually. Though the veil of the temple has now been rent and the Spirit of God dwells within believers, a continual worship gathering in no way displaces the reality of the indwelling Spirit; rather, it testifies of the Spirit's presence.

I'm not suggesting that every individual church operate in 24/7 worship and prayer. I do believe, however, that much can be gained if we consider the biblical precedent and how it may be applied to the Church across our cities. In the new covenant, we are individually temples of the Holy Spirit, and at the same time, we are being built *together* as a dwelling place of God (Eph. 2:22). When

we host God's presence in our communities through continual worship and prayer, we will truly experience the
habitation of God among us.

HISTORICAL ACCOUNTS OF NIGHT AND DAY PRAYER

Night and day prayer may be considered a relatively new or recent trend in the Body of Christ. However, there are multiple examples of communities of believers throughout church history who have practiced night and day prayer.

The earliest post-biblical examples are found in monastic communities. For over one thousand years, monasticism held a key role in shaping theology in the Church. As early as the fourth century, monks and nuns were regarded as an integral part of society throughout the developing world. The early monastic communities coined the phrase *laus perennis*, or perpetual prayer. Through the monastic tradition, night and day prayer was birthed in the Church age.

Some of the key figures who were instrumental in establishing the foundations of modern night and day prayer were Alexander the Sleepless, Comgall, and Ludwig von Zinzendorf. In this chapter, we will take a brief look at the lives of these and others who were the pioneers of night and day prayer as we know it.

Alexander the Sleepless

Alexander the Sleepless was an officer in the Roman army in the fourth century AD. While studying Scripture, he was pierced by Jesus' words to the rich young ruler: "Sell whatever you have and give to the poor, and you will have treasure in heaven; and come, take up the cross, and follow Me" (Mk. 10:21). In obedience to the word of the Lord, he sold all that he had, retired from the army, and spent the next several years of his life in solitude in the desert of Syria. After seven years of solitude, tradition states that he reappeared and set fire to a pagan temple. He was arrested and thrown in prison. While imprisoned, Alexander led the prison governor and his household to the Lord. Afterward, he was released and returned to his life in the desert, where he converted a band of robbers into devoted Christians. His converts became the core of his new monastic movement.

Around 400 AD, Alexander and approximately 300 of his monks moved to Constantinople where he had been educated earlier in life. In response to Paul's command to "pray without ceasing" (1 Thes. 5:17), he established *laus perennis* in the monastery of St. Mennas. He and his followers incurred persecution from the regional chief bishop, because they were a threat to the political structure of the organized church in Constantinople. The persecution caused them to relocate to Gomon at the mouth of the Black Sea, near modern-day Istanbul, Turkey. In Gomon, Alexander founded the monastic order of the Acoemetae, which is literally translated "the sleepless ones." The monks were divided into six choirs. The choirs were trained to sing continuously for four-hour shifts, and each choir took a daily, four-hour shift. The uninterrupted prayer and worship continued twenty-four hours a day. According to Nikolai Velimirovch, "Alexander disputed with heretics, worked miracles by the grace of God and grew old serving the Lord."[1] Alexander died there in 430 AD. However, the influence of the Acoemetae and *laus perennis* continued.

The most famous monastery that practiced *laus perennis* was Studion. It was established in Constantinople between 462–463 AD. Studion became a center of piety and learning for the entire region. Its central focus was night and day prayer.[2]

The Monastery of St. Maurice

The practice of *laus perennis* found its way to the Western church in 522 AD through the monastery of St. Maurice in Agaunum, Switzerland. In 286 AD, a legion of 7,000 Egyptian soldiers, under the command of Maurice de Valois, was called to assist the Roman emperor Maximian in suppressing a rebellion in Gaul (France). Legend has it that all of the soldiers under Maurice's command were Christians. On their way to Gaul, Maurice's legion encamped at Agaunum in Switzerland. There, they were ordered by the Roman authorities to sacrifice to the Roman gods and to the Emperor in petition for victory. Maurice and his legion refused. Because of their refusal, Maximian ordered the decimation of the entire legion. All 7,000 Egyptian Christians were martyred because they would not worship the Roman emperor and his false gods.[3]

[1]   Nikolai Velimirovch, "Prologue from Ohrid: July 3," Serbian Orthodox Church Diocese of Western America, http://www.westsrbdio.org/prolog/prolog.cgi.
[2]   International House of Prayer, "A Brief History of 24/7 Prayer," http://www.ihop.org/Articles/1000045365/International_House_of/About_Us/A_Brief_History.aspx.
[3]   *Catholic Encyclopedia*, "St. Maurice," (New York: Robert Appleton Company,

The accuracy of this story has been questioned. However, the legend of the Agaunum martyrs spread. Some years later, a monastery was established at Agaunum in memory of the sacrifice of Maurice's legion. Between 515 AD and 521 AD, King Sigismund of Burgundy (an old province of eastern and central France) gave a large sum of money to the monastery in order to ensure its success. In 522 AD, St. Maurice's Monastery instituted *laus perennis* after the tradition of the Acoemetae.[4] Choirs of monks rotated singing duties. This practice continued day and night until around 900 AD, and it influenced monasteries all over France and Switzerland.[5]

St. Patrick and the Vale of Angels

In 433 AD, St. Patrick journeyed to Ireland to preach the gospel to the Irish. He was followed by others who established monastic centers throughout Ireland. Christianity in much of the deteriorating Roman Empire had been established with bishops overseeing cities and metropolitan areas. However, Ireland had never been conquered by Rome and had no urban centers. The church in Ireland was unaffected by the fall of the Roman Empire, and monasteries soon became the primary influence upon Irish society.

According to the 12th-century monk Jocelin, Patrick once rested in a valley in Bangor, Ireland. He and his friends saw a vision of heaven. Jocelin says, "They held the valley filled with heavenly light, and with a multitude of heaven, they heard, as chanted forth from the voice of

1913), http://en.wikisource.org/wiki/Catholic_Encyclopedia_(1913)/St._Maurice.

4   "St. Maurice's Abbey," Wikipedia, http://en.wikipedia.org/wiki/St._Maurice%27s_Abbey.

5   "Laus Perennis," Wikipedia, http://en.wikipedia.org/wiki/Laus_perennis.

angels, the psalmody of the celestial choir."[6] The place became known as the *Vallis Angelorum*, or the Vale of Angels. About one hundred years later, a renowned monastery would be built there that would embrace *laus perennis* and greatly impact Europe.

Comgall and Bangor Monastery

The man who founded the monastery in Bangor was named Comgall. He was born in Ulster, Ireland in 517 AD. Initially, he was a soldier, but upon his release from military service, he took monastic vows and was educated for his new life as a monk. Comgall's presiding bishop encouraged him to plant a monastery in the famed Vale of Angels. He founded the Abbey at Bangor between 552 and 559 AD. It is interesting to note that the monastery at Bangor was not Protestant, nor was it Roman Catholic. It was Celtic Christian, so it was not presided over by the Roman Catholic diocese and did not practice Roman Catholic traditions.

At Bangor, Comgall instituted a rigid monastic rule of constant prayer and fasting. His strict rule attracted rather than repelled the masses. Thousands flocked to Bangor in order to experience Comgall's intensely-focused spiritual leadership. Three thousand monks from around Europe were divided into three choirs of 800 singers each. Each choir would sing for an eight-hour shift daily. During one of these shifts, four hundred monks would stand on one side of the auditorium while four hundred stood across from them as they sang in antiphonal response. Worship continued twenty-four hours a day, and each of the three shifts sang for eight hours. The choirs' antiphonal singing

[6] Jocelin, *The Most Ancient Lives of Saint Patrick*, (Charleston: BiblioBazaar, 2007 e-book).

was reminiscent of St. Patrick's vision of the heavenly choir some 120 years earlier.

Bangor Abbey became the epicenter of spiritual revival and education in Europe for the next 300 years. God's power was mightily displayed through the ministry of Comgall.[7] History records that he performed miraculous signs, wonders, and healings, and on one occasion he caused blindness to fall on a gang of thieves.[8]

The Monastery of Cluny

The ninth and tenth centuries were difficult times. The Vikings were ravaging Europe. Feudalism was on the rise. Monasteries were raided and subjugated by local chieftains. The Cluniac order was not only a reaction to these troubles; it was one of the most crucial reforms in the Western church.

William the Pious, the Duke of Aquitaine, founded the monastery at Cluny in 910 AD. He installed a man named Berno as the first abbot. William the Pious donated many of his personal resources, as well as his hunting preserve in the forests of Burgundy, to the monastery. This large endowment of resources allowed the abbey to be free from all secular financial and legislative entanglements. This autonomy enabled the monks to commit themselves to *laus perennis*.[9]

The second abbot, Odo, took over around 926 AD. He was zealous to see spiritual reformation touch not only the monastic orders but also the entire society of Europe,

---

[7] James MacCaffrey, "St. Comgall," The Catholic Encyclopedia, http://www. newadvent.org/cathen/04152c.htm.

[8] *Glimpses of Christian History*, "May 10, Annually: We Remember Irish Abbot Comgall," Christianity Today International, http://www.christianhistorytimeline.com/DAILYF/2002/05/daily-05-10-2002.shtml.

[9] Wikipedia, "Cluny Abbey," http://en.wikipedia.org/wiki/Cluny_Abbey.

and, under his leadership, that is exactly what happened.[10] Many smaller monastic houses, which looked to Cluny as their motherhouse, sprouted up throughout the land. Known for its independence, hospitality, and alms giving, the monastery at Cluny removed manual labor from a monk's daily responsibilities, replacing it with increased prayer. The Cluny Monastery reached its height of power and influence in the twelfth century, overseeing more than 300 monasteries all over Europe.[11]

Zinzendorf and the Moravians

Count Nicholas Ludwig von Zinzendorf was born in 1700 AD in Dresden, Germany. In 1722, Zinzendorf bought an estate in Berthelsdorf, Germany, from his grandmother, and offered refuge in his newly purchased estate to a group of persecuted Moravian Christians known as the Unitas Fratrum. These Moravians were the remnant following of the reformer John Huss. Since the 1600s, these saints had suffered under the hands of successive repressive Catholic monarchs.[12] On Zinzendorf's Berthelsdorf estate, they formed the community of Herrnhut, or "The Watch of the Lord." Herrnhut's population quickly grew to around three hundred. However, due to divisions and tension among the Moravians, Zinzendorf had to become the leader of the community and create a new spiritual constitution for the brethren.

On August 13, 1727, the power of God came down

---

[10] Wikipedia, "Odo of Cluny," http://en.wikipedia.org/wiki/Odo_of_Cluny.

[11] George C. Alston, "Congregation of Cluny," The Catholic Encyclopedia, Vol. 4 (New York: Robert Appleton Company, 1908), http://www.newadvent.org/cathen/04073a.htm.

[12] Wikipedia, "Moravian Church," http://en.wikipedia.org/wiki/Moravian_Church.

upon a prayer meeting in the Berthelsdorf church.[13] (This day is commonly referred to as the Moravian Pentecost.) The move of the Spirit was so profound among the members of the community that they stayed up all night, not wanting the power of God to wane. Within two weeks of the outpouring, twenty-four men and twenty-four women made a covenant to each pray one hour daily every day. Leviticus 6:13 became their banner scripture: "The fire must be kept burning on the altar continuously; it must not go out" (NIV). Soon seventy people had committed to pray. This prayer meeting grew and would continue unabated for the next 120 years![14]

From the prayer rooms of Herrnhut, the modern Protestant missions movement was birthed. The missionary zeal that possessed the Moravians was unprecedented in church history. For instance, Protestants typically send out one missionary for every five thousand members of their denomination. The Moravians, however, had a much more aggressive ratio, sending out 226 missionaries by the year 1776. That's one missionary for every sixty of their members![15] We will never know the full impact the Moravians had in world evangelism, but we do know that they strongly influenced William Carey, the father of modern missions,[16] as well as John Wesley.[17] The impact of this little community of persecuted believers, committed to seeking the face of God night and day, has truly been immeasurable.

[13] Unitas Fratrum, "Origin and Growth of the Unitas Fratrum," http://www.unitasfratrum.org/pages/origin_and_growth.html.
[14] International House of Prayer, "A Brief History."
[15] Ibid.
[16] William Carey University, "The Moravians," http://www.wmcarey.edu/carey/wmward/Misc%20html/moravian.html.
[17] Christianity Today Library, "The Moravians and John Wesley," http://www.ctlibrary.com/ch/1982/issue1/128.html.

In 1733, only six years after the night and day prayer meeting started in Herrnhut, a religious revival broke out in Northampton, Massachusetts, led by a thirty-year-old Presbyterian preacher named Jonathan Edwards. This revival was the initial spark of the First Great Awakening which swept through the United States and Europe. Did the night and day prayer from Herrnhut, Germany release something in the Spirit that prepared the earth for this First Great Awakening?

The Church has a rich heritage of night and day prayer. Historically, God has always raised up a devoted people of prayer to prepare the earth through intercession for the move of His Spirit. As we look at the contemporary prayer movement, we see this reality reflected and we are able to glimpse what God has ordained for this time in history.

NIGHT AND DAY PRAYER IN THE EARTH TODAY

Recently, as I inventoried the various prayer ministries that are emerging around the globe, I was struck by what I found. The viral expansion of so many substantial prayer initiatives is unprecedented. No continent is excluded. Many streams of Christianity are participating in this powerful phenomenon of perpetual prayer. Like the morning sun cresting the horizon, the prayer movement is just beginning to engulf the globe.

In this chapter, I want to draw your attention to several of the current expressions of night and day prayer as examples of this burgeoning movement. When these prayer ministries are seen all together, it becomes clear that the Lord has chosen this generation, in a way like no other, to weave together a tapestry of worship and prayer that spans the globe.

As we consider the current global prayer movement, we must ask ourselves, "Why?" Why now? Why is the Lord building prayer in such a vigorous way? What does the Lord have in store for the generation in which He initiates a global torrent of intercession, as He has in our day?

With these questions in mind, let's consider one of the
Lord's grand purposes for prayer as portrayed in Revelation chapter 5.

Bowls of Prayer

> Then He came and took the scroll out of the right
> hand of Him who sat on the throne. Now when
> He had taken the scroll, the four living creatures
> and the twenty-four elders fell down before the
> Lamb, each having a harp, and golden bowls full of
> incense, which are the prayers of the saints.
>
> —Revelation 5:7–8

John reports a stunning truth here. The prayers of the
saints not only come unobstructed to the throne; they also
fill golden bowls as incense before God. It's an awesome
thought that throughout all of history, each prayer of every saint has not only been heard, but has remained before
God as a perpetual petition. These prayers ever rise before
Him, ministering to His heart and beckoning Him to action.

God has placed an immeasurable dignity upon the
human race: He values our weak mutterings. He doesn't
hear our cries just to quickly dismiss them. God *delights* in
the prayers of His people. He keeps them before Him forever, like a betrothed stores away letters from her beloved,
holding them for the day of their fulfillment.

The fact that the bowls are full *before* Jesus takes the
scroll from the Father's hand demonstrates the essential
place of prayer at the end of the age. The scroll can be
considered God's end-time action plan. Jesus takes the
scroll from the Father and opens its seals to initiate the
judgments that will culminate with His second coming.

It is only *after* the bowls of prayer are full that Jesus takes the scroll and looses its seals. Think of it—when the bowls of our prayers have reached the tipping point, the events of the end of the age will unfold. The global prayer movement is the catalyst that causes God to initiate His end-time plans.

Isaiah declared that when the judgments of the Lord are unleashed upon the earth, people learn righteousness (Isa. 26:9). Through His perfect leadership, God will simultaneously release judgment and mercy to the earth through the instrument of our intercessions.

As displayed through this portrayal of prayer in Revelation 5, a day is coming when the golden bowls of prayer in heaven will be filled. Will our generation see the inception of this end-time drama? Today, with the global emergence of many night and day prayer ministries, it is reasonable to conclude that such a climax is closer than ever before.

Some Prayer Ministries with a Night and Day Focus

Prayer Mountain, Seoul, South Korea

In 1958, David Yonggi Cho founded the Yoido Full Gospel Church with only a handful of people in attendance. The church began to grow, adding 1,000 members within three years. By the early 1970s, the church had reached over 10,000 members. In 1973, the church founded Prayer Mountain, which was to serve as a secluded place for believers desiring to seek the Lord privately in prayer and fasting. With over 200 prayer grottoes available twenty-four hours a day, Prayer Mountain's daily ministry services and ceaseless worship and prayer began to attract thousands of visitors. It soon became an epicenter for intercession that sparked spiritual awakening throughout Seoul, Korea. Today, over one million people annually frequent the serene prayer center. As a result of Cho's prayer initiative, his church rapidly expanded. Now, decades after the conception of Prayer Mountain, Yoido Full Gospel Church has become the world's largest church, boasting over 830,000 members.[1]

Undoubtedly, Pastor Cho's earnest desire to see night and day prayer established in South Korea has paved the way for other ministries to enter the global prayer movement. It is likely that the incense rising to God from South Korea over the last several decades has helped give birth to the prayer movement that is sweeping the globe today.

International House of Prayer, Kansas City, Missouri, USA

In September 1999, a prayer meeting began in Kansas City and has yet to cease. A vision that was over fifteen years in the making became a reality at the International House of Prayer of Kansas City, led by Mike Bickle. Beginning with a "Gideon company" of intercessors who were committed to the mandate of ceaseless worship and prayer, this missional community has continued in unbroken worship-led prayer meetings to this day. Staffed by missionaries who have chosen intercession as their first activity of missions work, the prayer room now hosts thousands in weekly attendance.

Each week, eighty-four 2-hour prayer meetings are led by worship teams and attended by hosts of hungry believers seeking the Lord with prayer and fasting. This is the foundation of their ministry: to win the lost, heal the

---

[1]   Wikipedia, "Yoido Full Gospel Church," http://en.wikipedia.org/wiki/Yoido_Full_Gospel_Church.

sick, and make disciples as they labor alongside the larger Body of Christ to see the Great Commission fulfilled, to engage in works of justice, and to live as forerunners who prepare the way for the return of Jesus.[2]

As a result of this community's commitment to night and day prayer, hundreds of similar houses of prayer have sprung up around the world. As of this writing, there are similar houses of prayer throughout the United States and in many other nations, including Austria, Canada, China, Colombia, the Czech Republic, Germany, Israel, Kenya, Mexico, New Zealand, Romania, South Africa, Switzerland, Taiwan, Thailand, and the United Kingdom.

International House of Prayer, Atlanta, Georgia, USA

The International House of Prayer–Atlanta is one such community birthed out of the missions base in Kansas City. In February 2006, Atlanta became the second American city to host ceaseless, worship-led prayer. Intercessors and worshipers have since manned the prayer room every hour of every day at the International House of Prayer–Atlanta. The missions base in Atlanta closely resembles the IHOP–KC model, with two-hour sets of live worship continuing consecutively and covering all 168 hours of the week. The intercessors at IHOP–Atlanta intend to maintain a corporate 24/7 expression of prayer in their city until Jesus returns to the earth.[3]

24-7 Prayer International, London, UK

Started by a group of young people in Chichester,

---

[2]   International House of Prayer of Kansas City, "About Us," http://www.IHOP. org.

[3]   International House of Prayer–Atlanta, "History," http://ihop-atlanta.com/ en_history.html.

England in 1999, the initial prayer room was manned by individuals taking one-hour blocks of time, in succession, to cover twenty-four hours a day. What began as one prayer room in southern England exploded across the globe, spreading into ninety countries and spawning thousands of prayer rooms that have engaged in twenty-four-hour prayer watches for weeks and even months at a time.

The mission of 24-7 Prayer is to transform the world through movements and communities of Christ-centered, mission-minded prayer. By returning to the simplest, most basic things of the Christian life—fasting, prayer, outreach to the lost, and ministry to the oppressed—the movement has had a dramatic impact upon the Church across the globe. Through prayer, coupled with multiple evangelistic and justice initiatives, the goal of 24-7 is ultimately to transform society and turn the tide of youth culture. Their revolutionary approach to Christianity and culture has caused the media to take notice of the movement, featuring it in newspapers and magazines from *Rolling Stone* to *Reader's Digest*.[4]

TheCall, Kansas City, Missouri, USA

In September 2000, through a dramatic series of events, Lou Engle rallied believers to gather on the Mall in Washington, DC for a day of fasting and prayer for revival in America. TheCall did not publish lists of speakers or publicize big-name bands, but over 400,000 believers convened that day in a solemn assembly to pray for mercy on America.[5]

---

[4] 24-7 Prayer, "What Is 24-7 Prayer?" http://www.24-7prayer.com/about/what.
[5] TheCall, "About Us," http://thecall.com/Publisher/Article.
     aspx?ID=1000044250.

Since then, TheCall has hosted multiple gatherings in America and abroad that draw hundreds of thousands annually for a day of concentrated fasting and prayer. For example, on July 7th, 2007 (7/7/07) over 70,000 people gathered in Nashville to fast and pray that God would shift the tide of sexual perversion that has so gripped America over the last forty years. Each event is described as a solemn assembly, patterned after the biblical mandate found in Joel 2: "'Now therefore,' says the LORD, 'Turn to Me with all your heart, with fasting, with weeping with mourning . . . gather the people, sanctify the congregation, assemble the elders'" (vv. 12, 16).

TheCall, now based in Kansas City, continues to facilitate large prayer events and extended fasts worldwide. Hundreds of thousands have been mobilized in prayer and fasting through TheCall's events and various initiatives.

Global Day of Prayer, Cape Town, South Africa

The Global Day of Prayer is an annual event that organizes Christians worldwide to unite in a day of prayer and repentance. In July 2000, the Lord gave a South African businessman named Graham Power a vision to see South Africa unite in a day of repentance and prayer. In 2002, the vision expanded to encompass all of Africa; 2004 saw the invitation extended to the world. Since its initial meeting in 2001, the Global Day of Prayer has seen millions of Christians from 220 nations gather on the same day for a concert of prayer that spans the globe. Stadiums around the earth are filled with repentant believers petitioning heaven to heal their nations. Through superb administration and execution, the organization has been able to touch the far reaches of the globe and fuse together believers from all denominations across nearly every nation.[6]

Though the Global Day of Prayer only lasts for one day, the significance of the day should not be overlooked, nor underestimated. Through globalization, the GDOP team has accomplished something unprecedented in organizing a worldwide chorus of prayer and worship to Jesus. And, looking past the day of prayer itself, the GDOP team has mobilized millions into lifestyles of prayer.

Burn 24-7, Richardson, Texas, USA

Burn 24-7 is a young, traveling ministry seeking to plant sustainable prayer operations throughout the earth. Through its emphasis on the core practices of Christianity—worship and prayer—Burn 24-7 desires to see the communities it visits transformed by the power of God. In its short existence, the ministry has already touched hundreds of cities, towns, and villages around the world, establishing prayer centers in the spirit of the tabernacle of David.

Upon arrival in a city, the group organizes multiple groups to come together at a "burn," which is a twenty-four-hour or longer non-stop worship and prayer meeting, divided into two-hour shifts. The goal is to see these gatherings cause a spiritual shift in the regions in which they are held.

Burn 24-7's mobile planting focus provides the prayer movement with a necessary vehicle for the worldwide establishment of night and day prayer. The ministry desires to see praise given to the Lord from every corner of the earth.[7]

---

6   Global Day of Prayer, "History," http://www.globaldayofprayer.com/history. html.

7   Burn 24-7, "About," http://burn24-7.com/about.

Justice Houses of Prayer

Washington DC, Boston, New York City, San Diego, and San Francisco all host Justice Houses of Prayer. The JHOP communities operate on extensive prayer schedules and have a specific intercessory focus on modern issues of justice, from abortion to human trafficking. This ministry is closely associated with TheCall, praying daily for the specific initiatives TheCall targets in their larger corporate gatherings.

Succat Hallel, Jerusalem, Israel

Since 2004, hundreds of intercessors have taken their place in a Jerusalem-based prayer house that overlooks Mount Zion. They are contending night and day until Jerusalem is again made a praise in the earth (Is. 62:7). The house of prayer is named Succat Hallel, which is Hebrew for "tabernacle of praise." The Succat Hallel community hosts intercessors from over five continents and offers short-term internships.

God declares in Isaiah 62 that He will set up intercessors who will pray around the clock for Jerusalem and never hold their peace. These intercessors are likened to watchmen who take their place on the wall of prayer, crying out for Jerusalem, until the city shines in righteousness. Succat Hallel is a highly significant ministry, serving as a host to intercessors who can pray *on-site* for the city of Jerusalem.[8]

Luke18 Project, Kansas City, Missouri, USA

The Luke18 Project is a grassroots, equipping ministry, endeavoring to raise up young college-aged leaders in the

---

[8] Succat Hallel, "About Us," http://www.jerusalempraise.com/website/about.

prayer movement. Ultimately, the ministry desires to see a network of prayer ministries planted and unified in a chorus of worship and prayer to prepare the way for the Lord's return. The Luke18 Project teaches leaders on college campuses to carry the mandate of intercession at their institutions. With over 150 chapters and affiliates, the ministry is starting fires of intercession across the nation.[9]

Various Cities

Prayer ministries geared toward a sustainable expression of night and day prayer are beginning to surface in several cities across the earth. Hong Kong, for example, contains four different prayer ministries that endeavor to fulfill a 24/7 prayer schedule. London hosts a house of prayer operating on a significant prayer schedule, ultimately desiring to run perpetually. Bogota, Cairo, Chicago, Jakarta, Jerusalem, Pretoria, Tauranga, and many other cities host at least one 24/7-minded prayer ministry.

Night and Day Prayer: More than a Ministerial Trend

Without question, night and day prayer is proliferating in cities across the globe. Participation in these ministries is increasing, allowing for greater sustainability, and enabling prayer to penetrate every region of the earth.

As we observe this pattern, let us consider Jesus' question in Luke 18:8: "When the Son of Man returns, will He find faith on the earth?" We must see with prophetic vision that God is raising up night and day prayer across the earth for more than just starting an exciting ministerial trend. These prayer ministries serve a significant purpose.

---

[9] Luke18 Project, "About," http://www.ihop.org/Publisher/Article.
    aspx?ID=1000051907.

Night and day prayer *will* be preserved until Jesus comes, that He might find faith on the earth. Let our hearts be encouraged by the rapid escalation of continual prayer, and let us consider its profundity, for it has been divinely ordained and initiated in this hour.

As we examine the global spectrum of night and day prayer, it is important to consider Jesus' requisite for the release of justice. The Lord declares that He will release justice when His people cry out to Him night and day (Lk. 18:7–8). The fact that night and day prayer is being established at this time is a sure sign that God intends to release global justice in a way people have never seen.

SPEEDY JUSTICE (LUKE 18:1–8)

Then Jesus told his disciples a parable to show them that they should always pray and not give up. He said: "In a certain town there was a judge who neither feared God nor cared about men. And there was a widow in that town who kept coming to him with the plea, 'Grant me justice against my adversary.' For some time he refused. But finally he said to himself, 'Even though I don't fear God or care about men, yet because this widow keeps bothering me, I will see that she gets justice, so that she won't eventually wear me out with her coming!'" And the Lord said, "Listen to what the unjust judge says. And will not God bring about justice for his chosen ones, who cry out to him day and night? Will he keep putting them off? I tell you, he will see that they get justice, and quickly. However, when the Son of Man comes, will he find faith on the earth?"

—Luke 18:1–8, NIV

Throughout the Scriptures, certain passages function as beacons of light, greatly illuminating our path. They provide foundational understanding of the topics they discuss. The parable of the unjust judge is one such passage, offering us a cornerstone of revelation regarding prayer. In this chapter, we will consider this parable and its essential application to the end-time prayer movement.

The Purpose of the Parable

In Luke 17:22–37, Jesus describes the condition of the earth during the season of His return. Jesus then tells the parable of the unjust judge, concluding it by again referencing the time of His second coming (Luke 18:8). Though the parable is applicable to believers of every generation, it would be a mistake to ignore its obvious context. Therefore, we should primarily consider the parable as an admonition to believers on the earth just prior to the time of the Lord's return.

Though many parables don't explicitly state their purpose, here Luke tells us the two-fold reason Jesus spoke this parable: to get men to pray without ceasing, and to keep them from giving up. In the past, when reading through this text, I actually felt *discouraged* from prayer rather than *encouraged*. I had misunderstood Jesus' purpose in telling this story and therefore misinterpreted His words. I finally realized that if the parable was not encouraging me to persevere in prayer, I must be missing something.

The parable of the unjust judge, briefly paraphrased, is this. A certain individual had illegally defrauded a widow. This widow filed her complaint with the local judge, hoping for justice to be served. Instead, the judge did nothing. He was a godless man, unconcerned with the widow's plight. She repeatedly brought her case before him until finally, because of her persistence, he arrested the guilty one. Ultimately, the judge was not moved by compassion; he was moved by the widow's unyielding resolve and continuous requests.

Contrast Rather than Compare

At a glance, it may seem like the unjust judge represents the eternal Father and the widow is a picture of believers. However, Jesus is not giving us a straightforward comparison; instead, He is contrasting the two figures. God is not like the unjust judge; rather, He is the exact opposite. He is the God of perfect justice, the avenger of all who are defrauded (1 Thes. 4:6).

Similarly, the widow is not a picture of the Bride, but rather the antithesis. The Church is forever joined to Jesus, never to be widowed. The widow has no relationship or influence with the judge, whereas the Church's position with Jesus is established. We are seated with Him in heavenly places and are the very object of His favor and affection.

In literature, this type of comparison is known as an "a fortiori'" argument. The first example is given to illustrate the clear truth of the second. Jesus encourages us by saying, "Do you hear what the unjust judge said?" If a godless, unjust judge will actually execute justice on behalf a widow, how much more will God, who is enthroned on justice, vindicate His beloved ones who pray to Him night and day?

In contrast to the unjust judge, Jesus rhetorically asks, "Will not God bring about justice for His chosen ones . . .?

Will he keep putting them off?" The answer is clear—God will *not* put off His people who cry out to Him day and night. He *will* answer them speedily!

Let these truths sink deep down into your soul. God is not unjust, and you are not a spiritual widow. Though it may seem that you continue to cry out over the same issues with no discernible change, God hears your cry and is answering your prayer.

Jesus finishes the parable by asking an important question: "In the day that I return, will I find faith on the earth?" He is not questioning whether there will be people of faith alive at the time of His coming. Instead, He is *instructing* us with this question, specifically addressing the concepts introduced in the parable. He is actually saying, "I want My people to relentlessly contend *night and day* in prayer at the time of My return to the earth. Who will engage with My plan and not give up?"

The Fainting Spirit

One of the great challenges intercessors face is discouragement. Those who have prayed long hours know the pain of adjuring heaven, only to be met with delays and seemingly unanswered prayer. At times, burdens of intercession are incredibly weighty and urgent. When we don't immediately see answers, we are tempted to discount the effectiveness of our prayers. We judge our success by discernible results rather than by God's delight in our obedience.

At other times, intercessors' constant engagement in spiritual conflict causes weariness. We pray earnestly, neglecting to take care of our physical, emotional, and spiritual needs. Ultimately, we find ourselves exhausted and we lose faith in prayer. Both discouragement and fatigue are reasons we give up before we see the fruit of our intercession.

Jesus told this parable to give us a vision for perseverance. He wants us to press on in prayer and not lose heart. Jesus assures us that the Father will not move one moment too late. He will answer our cries, *speedily*. He admonishes us to persistently hammer away in intercession until we see breakthrough, rather than becoming discouraged by what seems to be a delayed response from God. The Father longs to execute justice for His people. The point is, when we cry out continually, we will see the answers to our prayers as we persevere by God's grace.

Understanding Justice

Jesus promised that that those who call upon Him will receive justice. But what does "justice" mean? What is He is actually promising?

Biblically, justice is God working on behalf of the orphan, the widow, the foreigner, the poor, and the oppressed (Ps. 146:7–9). Another simple definition is "God making all the wrong things right."

Injustice has caused great harm to many. Issues such as human trafficking, abortion, poverty, and fatherlessness plague societies in every sphere of the globe. Additionally, there are grievous spiritual injustices, including sickness, disease, and demonic oppression. Ultimately, justice is *liberty to all who are captive*. God longs to be gracious to us—to rid the earth of its injustices and bring healing and salvation to all who are oppressed.

Night and Day As a Prerequisite

In the parable, Jesus tells us the necessary requirement

for seeing justice released. He says He will release justice when His people seek Him *night and day*. Many desire to see God move in great acts of justice, but they overlook this prescribed requisite.

In the generation the Lord returns, there will be more injustices in the earth than ever before (Dan. 8:23, 2 Tim. 3:1–5). God's antidote to offset this wickedness is night and day prayer. As His people engage His heart, bringing before Him cries for action, He will answer with power. Isaiah declared that He will return with aggression in His heart and will bring justice to every sphere of every society in the earth (Isa. 42:2–4). He intimately knows the plight of every person who's ever been victimized. He will not let one injustice remain unaddressed. He will make all the wrong things right, heal every wounded heart, and vindicate all who have been abused. When He comes, He will see to it that justice prevail throughout the earth (Ps. 72:2–4, 98:9; Isa. 11:4–5, 16:5).

This is why He has called us to pray night and day. He spoke this parable to encourage us to contend without quitting. He's given us the necessary ingredients to see massive breakthrough in our cities that will culminate in His second coming. If this is His promise, how shall we not hurl ourselves into the fray, praying until justice is established? Let's partner with His heart until we see every vestige of corruption expelled. Let's give ourselves to prayer night and day until righteousness reigns and justice rolls like a mighty river.

GOD'S PLAN FOR ISRAEL'S SALVATION (ISAIAH 62:1-5)

For Zion's sake I will not hold My peace, and for Jerusalem's sake I will not rest, until her righteousness goes forth as brightness, and her salvation as a lamp that burns.

—Isaiah 62:1

God's heart for justice is one of the primary reasons He is raising up an end-time global prayer movement. Yet another issue burns in the heart of the eternal Father, one that many of us in the Church do not fully understand. It is so important to Him that He declared through the prophet Isaiah that He would not hold His peace nor rest until His desire regarding this issue was manifest in the earth. He will not relent until this yearning of His heart is fulfilled. What is the cause of such passion? It is the salvation of the nation of Israel.

For many years I didn't understand what the Scriptures declared regarding God's plan for Israel. I had heard that Israel was important to Christianity and that we, as Christians, needed to pray for the peace of Jerusalem. Yet I had no real understanding of what this entailed. Only within the last several years have I begun to comprehend God's zeal over this people who seem to be continually at the center of international controversy.

To truly know God's heart, we must understand what is in His mind regarding the nation of Israel. By the inspiration of the Holy Spirit, Paul declared that all Israel would be saved (Rom. 11:25–26). Paul wanted to inform the Roman believers of God's plan to save the remnant of Israel at the end of the age. All believers must comprehend that God has a plan for His chosen people that includes the salvation of every Jew who will be alive on the planet at the time of Jesus' return. Never before has the earth seen a nation that is 100 percent born again. Yet, in the generation in which the Lord returns, all Israel shall be saved. This reality is burning on the Lord's heart, and He wants our hearts to burn with His—to love the people He loves and pray for their salvation. This is the nation upon whom He has set His affections.

It's important that we understand that God has chosen Israel for Himself. But we must also comprehend *why* He has chosen this people. In His eternal purposes, God most likely has more reasons than we truly understand. However, I will mention several here that are evident to us from the Scriptures.

Sovereign Election

Psalm 113:6 declares that our God humbles Himself when He beholds things in heaven and earth. Consider the greatness of our God: He is so superior to all created things that it is dramatically humbling for Him to even *look* upon His creation. He is highly exalted over all His works. He is the Sovereign God of the entire universe. All things came into being and are held together by His very word.

His ways and thoughts are far superior to ours. In this age, we are only able to understand a small fragment of His plans. Yet, at the same time, the things that we *are* able to comprehend are enough to thrill us all the days of our lives.

God's eternal purposes are beyond our comprehension. He continually makes decisions according to His sovereign plans, and the reasoning behind His plans is not apparent to us because we lack the information that only He possesses. He knows *everything* and accomplishes *everything* that He desires in perfection according to His eternal purposes. Ultimately, His ways and decisions are infinitely higher than our own.

In this age, even the most spiritually sensitive, prophetic person sees through a glass darkly when pondering God's choice of Israel. It is God's choice and privilege to reveal to us or to veil from us whatever He desires. Undoubtedly, God's election and choice of Israel has manifold purposes that we cannot and will not fully comprehend in this age. He is the Sovereign God who operates all things flawlessly. Since He is perfect and all that He does is perfect, we can ascertain that His choice of Israel is perfect.

A Special Treasure

In God's address to Israel at the onset of the exodus from Egypt, we find the first of several reasons for His choice.

Now therefore, if you will indeed obey My voice and keep My covenant, then you shall be a special treasure to Me above all people.

—Exodus 19:5

God chose the people of Israel to be a "special treasure" to Him. The New International Version translates
the phrase as "treasured possession." At times we overlook
the fact that God yearns for intimacy with people. His
heart burns with passion to give and to receive love. He
Himself *is* love, and therefore He *must* love. Love that
does not give is not love at all. He had to selflessly give
love to ones who had the option of rejecting His love.
God has always desired intimacy with all the people of
His creation.

When He carried Israel out of Egypt so that they
might worship Him in the desert, we see the very core of
God's desire for all the nations. He chose Israel to be a
people who would voluntarily love Him and demonstrate
to all the earth His desire for intimacy with all mankind.
He wanted a people with whom He could express the affections of His heart as a template for relationship with
the rest of creation.

God's foremost motivation for everything that He
does is love. Therefore, when He chose the nation of Israel, He chose them because of love. They were the unde-
serving recipients of His heavenly affections. Though they
have almost totally rejected their Messiah, when He returns, they will turn from their hardness of heart, and with
weeping and repentance, embrace Him as their King and
their God (Zech. 12:10). They will be the example to all
the earth of what it means to live as God's special treasure.

Kingdom of Priests

> And you will be for Me a kingdom of priests and
> a holy nation.
>
> —Exodus 19:6

God wanted Israel to be a nation whose entire purpose was to be a priesthood unto Him. Because God
longs for intimacy, He wanted to give His people access
to His heart and His emotions. He desires to give and
receive love from men. Just as priests are called to stand
before God and bless Him with worship and adoration,
Israel was to serve the Lord as a kingdom of priests—as
a nation who would not only minister to God's heart, but
would also minister *on behalf* of God to the hearts of men.

God raised up Israel as an example of what He would
do for the nation whose people would fully give themselves to Him. He declared to Israel that He would bless
them abundantly if they would serve and obey Him (Deut.
28). By separating this people unto Himself and blessing
them greatly, He would provoke all nations of the earth to
seek this same intimacy with their Father.

Never has the earth seen an entire nation whose people have given themselves completely in abandonment to
God. However, in the coming age, all Israel will be possessed with the "spirit of burning," completely filled with
passion and desire for the Lord (Isa. 4:4). They will serve
the Lord with fervent zeal. In that day, the nations of the
earth will be drawn to them because the glory of the Lord
will rest upon them (Isa. 60:1–5). Isaiah declares that in
that day, the abundance of the nations will be converted
because of Israel's righteous testimony (Isa. 60:5; Hos.
2:23; Zech. 8:23).

A Lineage for Messiah

When Adam fell into sin through Satan's lure, he forfeited intimacy with God on behalf of all mankind. But God immediately initiated an action plan to redeem the entire human race. God declared that a man would be born who would restore intimacy with God for all mankind and overcome Satan by crushing his head (Gen. 3:15, NIV). That Man is Jesus—the Jewish carpenter from Nazareth—the Messiah. The Bible declares that Jesus disarmed every demonic force and triumphed over the enemy through the victory of the cross (Col. 2:15).

Since it was a man who forfeited intimacy with God, it was necessary for God to use a man to restore that intimacy. That man had to be born through a woman. In other words, he had to actually be human. For him to have the power to redeem mankind, he had to have the ability to choose either righteousness or wickedness, and to meet the requirement of living a sinless life (Heb. 4:15, 7:26–27). Jesus met that requirement, and now, through His blood, we have free access to the throne of God. But Jesus has not only restored us to intimacy with the eternal Father; He has also destroyed the works of the enemy in our lives.

While we understand that Jesus is God, sometimes we forget that He is also a man. He did not just momentarily become a man and then return to being God after His resurrection. When He became a man, He became a man for eternity. He is fully God and fully man, forever. He sits, as a man, at the right hand of the Father to intercede for the rest of humanity. He is the perfect representative of God to man, and of man to God. While He lived on the earth, He experienced all the challenges and temptations that we go through. And so He is easily able to sympathize with our weaknesses (Heb. 4:15). He has been tempted in every way that we are, yet is without sin.

Since God determined to send His Son to the earth as a man, He had to choose a people through whom His Son would be born. In His sovereignty, God chose Abraham and formed the nation of Israel through his lineage. One of the divine purposes of this nation was to birth Messiah. How amazing to think that when God chose Abraham, He chose him so that He could bring forth Jesus through Abraham's seed! No wonder He is zealous for Israel with such great zeal!

God's Passion for Israel

> The Gentiles shall see your righteousness, and all kings your glory. You shall be called by a new name, which the mouth of the LORD will name. You shall also be a crown of glory in the hand of the LORD, and a royal diadem in the hand of your God.
> —Isaiah 62:2–3

Isaiah 62 is an extremely important chapter regarding God's end-time plan for Israel and how He will use night and day prayer to bring His purposes to pass. Perhaps no other verses in the Bible describe with such clarity God's desire for Israel. Here God clearly enumerates His strategy to make Zion "a praise in the earth" (v. 7).

God is zealous to see Israel burning with righteousness and salvation. In that day the people of Israel will be a "crown of glory in the hand of the Lord" (v. 3). God is the perfection of beauty. He "wraps himself in light as a garment" (Ps. 104:2, NIV). What kind of crown could possibly adorn the One who is beauty Himself? Isaiah conveys the idea that Israel will burn with righteousness and glory to such an extent that they will be beautiful not only to the Lord, but also to the nations of the earth.

> You shall no longer be termed Forsaken, nor shall your land any more be termed Desolate; but you shall be called Hephzibah, and your land Beulah; for the LORD delights in you, and your land shall be married.
>
> —Isaiah 62:4

The Lord Himself is going to give the people of Israel a new name. Rather than being called "forsaken," they shall be called "Hephzibah;" literally, "the one in whom the Lord delights." God has always delighted in His people. Though they rejected their Messiah at His first coming, God has continued to call them *His* people (Rom. 11:2). When He gives them their new name, all the earth will know that this is the nation in whom God delights.

Before Jesus returns, Antichrist's armies will devastate Israel (Joel 3:2, 12; Zeph. 3:8; Zech. 12:2–3, 14:2; Rev. 16:14), and the nations of the earth will consider her forsaken by the Lord. Yet God will not leave Israel in that state. Isaiah declares that rather than being considered desolate, they shall be called "Beulah;" literally, "married." God will heal Israel's land, and all the nations of the earth will know Israel as the people who are married to the Lord. What a dramatic turnaround is in store for this nation!

> For as a young man marries a virgin, so shall your sons marry you; and as the bridegroom rejoices over the bride, so shall your God rejoice over you.
>
> —Isaiah 62:5

God will rejoice over Israel in the same way that a newly married bridegroom rejoices over and delights in his bride. God does not call Israel to salvation simply to fulfill a contractual obligation; He is deeply in love with His people, passionately longing for them. When they come to the knowledge of Jesus as Messiah, they will experience the full measure of God's great passion and joy over them. In that day, His eternal desire for them will be fulfilled. They will give Him their love with abandoned zeal. This is a non-negotiable plan in the Lord's heart. He is burning with desire to see Israel fully in love with His Son; He is committed to and focused on the salvation of this nation.

Today many of the people of Israel are socially "Jewish" but religiously agnostic. However, one day every nation will regard Israel as the picture of righteousness, burning with passion for her Messiah. In that day all the nations of the earth will be instructed by Israel's example. Isaiah 60:3 declares that all the nations of the earth will be drawn to Israel because of her light and beauty. She will be a crown of glory to the Lord, a royal diadem for all to see. God's plan for her redemption is established and He will not rest until it comes to pass. Since God's desire is so fully established in regard to this nation, we must ask ourselves, "What part do we have to play in this plan?"

SET WATCHMEN (ISAIAH 62:6–7)

I have set watchmen on your walls, O Jerusalem;
they shall never hold their peace day or night. You
who make mention of the LORD, do not keep si-
lent, and give Him no rest till He establishes and
till He makes Jerusalem a praise in the earth.

—Isaiah 62:6–7

As we discussed in the previous chapter, the first five
verses of Isaiah 62 clearly identify God's fervent desire to see all Israel saved. He is burning for her salvation
and He will not relent. Verses 6 and 7 contain God's plan
to see this desire come to pass.

Set Watchmen

The Lord declares that He has set "watchmen" on the
walls of Jerusalem who will never hold their peace, day or
night. These watchmen are at the center of God's strategy
to bring about the full salvation of Israel.

Historically, watchmen were set upon city walls or
upon nearby hills to look out for impending danger. They
worked with gatekeepers, who were stationed as operators

of the city gates. Watchmen had to have keen vision so that they could identify an approaching envoy or entourage. They could tell, even from far away, if those approaching were friend or foe. Once the watchmen identified who was approaching, they would instruct the gatekeepers to either open or lock the gates. If they sensed a threat to the city, the watchmen would send a warning to the king or the head of the military so that the army could address the impending danger.

In these verses, the Lord uses watchmen and walls as symbols. Watchmen represent intercessors. Just as watchmen gaze into the distance to see any who approach, God's people pray and receive insight regarding His plans. Similarly, when Isaiah declares that God has set watchmen "upon the walls of Jerusalem," the phrase "upon the walls" is not to be understood as an actual location; rather, it conveys the focus of God's attention: Israel. The watchmen are therefore commissioned by God to pray that His desire concerning Israel comes to pass.

Historically, watchmen operated in battalions that worked in shifts, covering the city from sunrise to sunset and all through the night. Similarly, the Lord prophesied through Isaiah that He would raise up watch*men*, plural—communities in which intercessors would engage in prayer night and day. These communities will never cease praying until salvation comes to all of Israel.

The next part of these verses identifies the watchmen as ones "who make mention of the Lord." The NIV translates this phrase as ones "who call out to the Lord." There can be no question, then, that these watchmen are intercessors who continually cry out to the Lord in prayer.

One of the most powerful aspects of Isaiah 62:6 is that

it is written in the past tense. God says, "I *have set* watchmen on your walls." Our God is the God who sees the end from the beginning. The night and day prayer movement in the earth is only beginning, but it will become much greater in scope and power in the coming decades. Before the end of this age, communities all over the globe will cry out to the Lord in night and day prayer for the salvation of Israel. *This is an already-established reality in God's heart that will surely come to pass.*

Who Are These Watchmen?

How does one know if he or she is called to be "set" as a watchman? Most who feel specifically drawn to prayer or worship don't think of themselves as watchmen for Jerusalem's salvation. All they really know is that they desire to spend long hours with the Lord.

Years ago, as a youth pastor gripped with a passion for revival, I had no idea of God's plan for Israel's salvation. All I knew was that I had an insatiable hunger for God to move in power in my life —and the way to see that happen was through prayer. For years the Lord had prophetically spoken to me about being a watchman and a gatekeeper, but I had no idea what those words meant. The name of our youth ministry, "212," even spoke of the number of gatekeepers in the tabernacle of David (1 Chr. 9:22). But even though I was familiar with that verse, I did not realize what the Lord was declaring over me.

Only *after* God dealt with me about transitioning from youth ministry into planting a house of prayer did I realize He had called me to be an Isaiah 62 watchman. In reality, He had been preparing me for this mandate my entire Christian life. When that realization touched my heart, I understood what God had been saying all along. I had been "set."

Though the entire Bible is anointed and divinely powerful, it is common for us to choose certain passages that "speak" to us as our favorites. But there is a vast difference between a passage that speaks *to* you and a passage that speaks *about* you. I was exhilarated the first time I realized that those who are a part of the current night and day prayer movement are actually a living fulfillment of God's prophetic promise in Isaiah 62. Was God speaking of me over 2,700 years ago when Isaiah prophesied these words?

Never before in history has God commissioned a global company of believers to devote their lives to night and day prayer. The number of people who feel led to serve the Lord in this fashion is rapidly growing. I believe Isaiah 62 is specifically written about those who, in this hour of history, are heeding the call to cry out day and night until Zion is made a praise in the earth. Do you sense the Lord's leading hand upon your heart? Could it be that you are also part of this watchmen company of whom Isaiah prophesied?

Though many look for supernatural signs from heaven to confirm God's leading in their lives, more often God's calling does not generally manifest via a supernatural visitation. So how do you know if God is "setting" you as a watchman? Perhaps you feel led by the Lord to take a season of your life to serve God in prayer and fasting as your main focus. Is it possible that the reason you feel nudged in this direction is because God is raising up a global prayer movement? God sets a person as a watchman when that person simply realizes that God is calling him to prayer as his primary pursuit. When this truth is revealed to the heart, it is a supernatural work of God's grace. Divine revelation upon our hearts is the primary way that God leads us into any calling. And it is the principle way that He "sets" watchmen.

People can't manufacture the desire to spend their lives in intercession and worship. To the contrary, the Scripture tells us there is "none who seeks God" (Rom 3:11). Anyone who has this desire burning within him is a living emblem of the grace of God working on the human heart. The likely reason you want to give yourself to night and day prayer is because God is wooing you to partner with His end-time agenda.

Never Hold Their Peace

God says in Isaiah 62:1 that He will not rest nor hold His peace until Israel burns with His very righteousness. In the same way, those who are set as watchmen will not rest nor hold *their* peace until Zion becomes a praise in the earth. God is giving zeal to His end-time church so that we will cry out in intercession, empowered by His very passions for Israel. How else could broken, frail humans accomplish the massive feat of ceaselessly interceding unto the fulfillment of God's divine purpose? In His grace and by His zeal, the end-time church will cry out night and day. We will never hold our peace!

The global prayer movement will not only operate in God's passion, but also in a way that mirrors worship in the heavenly throne room: night and day on earth just as it is in heaven. God does not rest; therefore, He is raising up a people who, likewise, will not rest, but who will be moved with His great passions in full cooperation with His plans.

Jerusalem: A Praise in the Earth

Though the prayer movement is still in its infancy compared to what it will be, the fact that it is emerging is a prophetic indicator that we are living in the season of the fulfillment of Isaiah 62. Let this truth cause your heart to tremble. Who but God alone could mastermind a plan to bring night and day prayer to the forefront of the Body of Christ across the globe?

Just as God has already set watchmen on the walls of Jerusalem, so too He has already established the prophecy that Jerusalem will become a praise in the earth. What does it mean for Jerusalem to become "a praise in the earth?" It is not simply that she will experience prosperity and peace, or that all of her inhabitants will be saved, although those things will take place. When the Lord says that Jerusalem will become "a praise in the earth," He is referring to a far greater reality. The only way that Jerusalem will become praiseworthy is when One who is worthy of praise is dwelling in her midst. Thus, He is referring to the day when Jesus' throne will be established in Jerusalem, making her the praise of the whole earth.

The Scriptures are full of verses declaring Jerusalem as the chosen dwelling of the Lord forever (Ps. 48:1–8, 50:1–3, 132:13; Isa. 60; Zech. 1:14–17, 2:5, 10–12, 8:1–8). When Jesus returns to the planet, He is coming to set up His global empire—to establish the kingdom of God on the earth. Then and only then will Jerusalem truly be "a praise in the earth." Jesus will rule the planet from Jerusalem, and the nations of the earth will come there every year to worship the Lord (Zech. 14:16). Isaiah 2:3 tells us that people will stream to Jerusalem to hear Jesus teach the ways of the Lord. How awesome it will be when our

King, Jesus, proclaims God's laws from Zion! Zechariah 2:5 declares that Jesus will be the glory in the midst of Jerusalem. Oh, for the day that we see this with our own eyes!

KINGDOM COME

After observing the prayer lives of John the Baptist's disciples, Jesus' own twelve asked for a lesson on prayer. "Teach us to pray, as John also taught his disciples," they asked. Jesus' response is now echoed in church services on a weekly basis worldwide.

> Our Father in heaven, hallowed be Your name. *Your kingdom come. Your will be done, on earth as it is in heaven.* Give us day by day our daily bread. And forgive us our sins, for we also forgive everyone who is indebted to us. And do not lead us into temptation, but deliver us from the evil one.
> —Luke 11:2–4, emphasis added

The Lord's Prayer serves as an important example of prayer. However, because of Christians' familiarity with it, we often mutter the prayer without considering the importance of its words. At the crux of this prayer lies a familiar but incredibly fearsome concept.

In Jesus' primary teaching on prayer, He instructs His disciples to petition the Father for His kingdom to come and His will to be done on the earth, in the same way as it is in heaven. In heaven there is no breach in God's full sovereign reign and authority. There is not a moment of indecision among the heavenly hosts. Everything operates fully and completely by the ever-guiding direction of the Creator. When we request that this type of rule be instituted in the earth, we must be prepared for God to intrude upon our own lives, at the least, and thoroughly devastate us, at the most. When we pray "Your kingdom come; Your will be done," we must understand that we are surrendering our kingdom and our will.

Let us reconcile Jesus' lesson in prayer with our own view of prayer's purpose. Popular preaching often portrays prayer as the means to an end that ultimately serves the needs of the one praying. However, Jesus' instruction depicts prayer as an ongoing necessity if we are to see *God's will* fully established on earth.

Rather than parroting liturgical jargon when we pray, we need to understand God's kingdom and what it means to pray in accordance with His divine intentions. God's agenda for prayer is far greater than our own petty purposes. He fully intends to answer the prayers of His people and ultimately establish His kingdom in every facet of every society. According to the prayer lesson that Jesus Himself gave the disciples, this intention must be our principal consideration in intercession. Let us, then, examine more closely the comprehensive establishment of the kingdom.

The History of the Kingdom

From the time of creation, God ordained His kingdom to one day cover the earth. The "kingdom come" will cause the culture of heaven to permeate every earthly society with righteousness and justice. Additionally, out of His great desire to partner with human beings, God has always intended that man would rule His kingdom and have dominion throughout the globe. To understand and embrace God's final plan for the establishment of His kingdom on earth, it is helpful to trace its development from Adam until now.

Adam

God gave Adam full dominion over the earth and its inhabitants. In doing so, He established Adam as the first man in charge of His kingdom on earth. However, when Adam sinned by disobeying God, he forfeited his earthly authority and dominion, handing them over to Satan.

Abraham

Approximately 2,000 years after Adam's fall, God set apart Abram to begin the process of restoring man's place in His kingdom. His plan was to bring forth a nation, later called Israel, from Abram. God changed Abram's name to Abraham and told him that the number of his descendants would be greater than the stars in the sky. God's intricate plan included one day uniting the kingdom of Israel's descendants with the kingdom of God—a future king of Israel would be the chosen ruler of His kingdom on the earth.

David

About 1,000 years passed from the time that God called Abraham until the time that Israel's second king, David, reigned (around 1000 BC). After David became king, God prophesied that David would be part of an incredible family dynasty. In fact, God promised that *all* the kings of Israel would come from David's line. Further, God's own Son, Messiah, would come from the seed of David and would one day reign forever.

> Furthermore I tell you that the LORD will build you a house. And it shall be, when your days are fulfilled, when you must go to be with your fathers, that I will set up your seed after you, who will be of your sons; and I will establish his kingdom. He shall build Me a house, and I will establish his throne forever. I will be his Father, and he shall be My son; and I will not take My mercy away from him, as I took it from him who was before you. And I will establish him in My house and in My kingdom forever; and his throne shall be established forever.
>
> —1 Chronicles 17:10–14

David was the first king to rule the empire over which the Son of God will one day reign forever. It's hard to believe, but God promised David that His own Son would rule and reign not only over the nation of Israel, but over God's kingdom on earth. As king of Israel, David knew that he was sitting on God's earthly throne. David actually referred to his own throne as "the throne of the kingdom of the Lord" (1 Chr. 28:5, 29:23)!

Daniel

After David's death, his son Solomon ruled Israel. But it wasn't long before Solomon disobeyed God by setting up idols from neighboring nations. As a result, the kingdom of Israel was eventually split in two, and the people began to turn away from God. Within 400 years, they were completely decimated—carried away to Babylon in exile. Because Israel was no more, it looked as if there was no hope for God's chosen king to ever sit upon Jerusalem's eternal throne.

In Babylon, God raised up Daniel as a prophet to explain His plan regarding Israel's future and the reign of the future king.

> I was watching in the night visions, and behold, One like the Son of Man, coming with the clouds of heaven! He came to the Ancient of Days, and they brought Him near before Him. Then to Him was given dominion and glory and a kingdom, that all peoples, nations, and languages should serve Him. His dominion is an everlasting dominion, which shall not pass away, and His kingdom the one which shall not be destroyed.
>
> —Daniel 7:13–14

Daniel's vision gave hope to captive Israel that Messiah was still coming, despite the fact that the nation was in captivity. These visions became a source of significant encouragement for Israel, giving them renewed hope in the earthly establishment of God's kingdom.

John the Baptist

John, the cousin of Jesus, was the forerunner of the coming king. His message could be summed up with one thought: "Repent, because the kingdom of God is here, now!" John declared to Israel that the kingdom was beginning upon the earth, telling the ordained inheritors that they must change their lifestyles and the way they understood the kingdom if they were to receive it. John proclaimed that merely being the chosen bloodline would not gain them entrance into the kingdom of God, for *all* men had given their allegiance to the kingdom of darkness. John boldly warned Israel that her sins disqualified her from citizenship in the Lord's kingdom. She must now heed God's requirement of repentance to enter and participate in the kingdom.

Jesus

At the beginning of His public ministry, Jesus also proclaimed the coming kingdom and told people to repent of their sins. He manifested the kingdom's power through signs and wonders, confirming the authenticity of His claims that He was the Son of God. The Pharisees thought they could end Jesus' destiny by having Him crucified, but Christ's crucifixion was the very act that forever sealed His rulership. Through His death and resurrection, He opened God's kingdom to all who would renounce the values of the kingdom of darkness and embrace the values of the kingdom of God.

Jesus won back the authority that Adam had lost. This is Paul's reason for presenting Jesus as the last Adam (Rom. 5:14). Jesus has received all authority to institute His kingdom upon the earth, and He has called His Church to disciple the nations in the values and principles of the kingdom of God. Our role is to establish the kingdom throughout the earth until the day Jesus comes to finalize its completion.

The kingdom of God is not an abstract reality. Jesus is returning not simply to fulfill the promise made to David, but to see His Father's will physically enacted on earth as it is in heaven. When Jesus returns, He will rule all nations as God's chosen King. He will take dominion and institute the kingdom of God throughout the earth. Every facet of society in every nation will be ruled by Jesus and embrace His value system.

Revelation 20 is the most well-known passage on the subject, but Scripture is full of verses referring to the reality of the returning King.[1] Daniel prophesied of a man "coming with the clouds of heaven . . . To Him was given dominion and glory and a kingdom, that all peoples, nations, and languages should serve Him" (Dan. 7: 13–14). Jesus is returning in power to rule over an everlasting kingdom, on earth as it is in heaven.

The Necessity of Repentance

One does not have to wait until Christ's return before entering the kingdom of God. The way into God's kingdom is open now and He has extended an invitation for all to enter. However, entrance is conditional upon repentance. To repent is to change one's mind unto changing his actions. It is not good enough to only "feel sorry." That sorrow must lead to a change in behavior. To truly repent, one must turn away from darkness and turn to God's light. When a person renounces his citizenship in the kingdom of darkness, confesses his sins, and chooses to submit himself fully to the values of the kingdom of God, only then does he truly enter in.

Forgiveness is often preached without calling people to repentance. People run to receive mercy from God, yet they receive nothing, for there is no entrance to the kingdom of God without true repentance. They must voluntarily turn

[1] E.g., Isaiah 2, 4, 11–12, 35; Jeremiah 33; Ezekiel 40–43; Zephaniah 3; and Zechariah 2. For more passages on the end times, see the International House of Prayer, "150 Chapters on the End Times," http://www.ihop.org/Articles/1000042608/International_House_of/Ministries/onething/Resources/Articles/150_Chapters_on.aspx.

from darkness to be able to accept the offer of forgiveness through Christ's blood and enter the kingdom. People's consciences become seared when they are offered forgiveness without the requirement of repentance. They believe themselves to be saved, yet they continue in sin. If a person never leaves the kingdom of darkness, how can he enter the kingdom of light?

The repentance message is central to the gospel of the kingdom. Jesus identified the proclamation of this message as an important catalyst for His return (Mt. 24:14). Once the gospel of the kingdom is preached to all nations, Jesus will come and take possession of the earth.

God's Agenda

> I have set My King on My holy hill of Zion.
> —Psalm 2:6

God has made up His mind that Jesus is to be His chosen King on earth. Though the nations rage against God's choice (Ps. 2:1–3), His is the only vote that matters. Jesus is coming to initiate a global takeover. Though the kingdom of darkness currently prevails over the nations, a new kingdom has been inaugurated and is coming in fullness. In His mercy, right now He is extending an invitation to *every* nation to repent before He completes the establishment of God's kingdom on the earth.

Jesus' worldwide empire will be far greater than any human empire that has ever existed. He will institute the value system of His kingdom throughout the earth. Every nation will participate harmoniously in God's government, choosing righteousness over wickedness. And Jesus, as King of kings, will fully restore humanity's loyalty to God through His 1,000-year reign of righteousness and justice.

After this 1,000-year reign (known as the Millennium), the earth will be restored—realigned with God's holy ways. Paul says it this way: "He must reign till He has put all enemies under His feet . . . when all things are made subject to Him, then the Son Himself will also be subject to Him who put all things under Him, that God may be all in all" (1 Cor. 15:25, 28). God will make His tabernacle with men, and the bliss of Eden will again be realized—this time on a global scale.

These plans are not negotiable. The Father's intentions are already determined. He will not be influenced or intimidated. No man's opinion will cause Him to relent. He has already chosen Jesus to be the human leader of the kingdom of God on the earth.

This is a key issue on the Father's end-time agenda, and it is the very reason that Jesus instructed us to pray for the earthly establishment of God's kingdom when He taught us the Lord's Prayer. In essence, the Church has been petitioning heaven to institute Jesus' earthly reign for over 2,000 years!

What's more staggering is that the global prayer movement that God is raising up right now focuses on Jesus' return and the coming of God's kingdom. Never before in the history of the earth has God raised up a corporate, night-and-day cry for Jesus to return. This global symphony of prayer is beginning to move in harmony with the Father's will. With one voice and in unity with the Holy Spirit, the Bride is crying out, "Come, Lord Jesus" (Rev. 21:17, 20).

It is amazing to consider that millions around the world are petitioning Jesus to come, fulfill the Father's plan, and take authority over the planet. He is going to answer this corporate cry in a definitive way. This is God's agenda, and right now the prayer movement is "hastening the coming of the day of God" (2 Pet. 3:12), contending until the kingdom of God is fully established upon the earth. Your kingdom come, Your will be done, on earth as it is in heaven!

THE GREAT DRAMA OF THE AGES

Now that we understand that Jesus is returning in answer to His people's prayers and that He will establish God's kingdom throughout the earth, it begs the question, "How will this incredible drama unfold?"

Great conflict is on the horizon. The forces of darkness and the forces of light are going to collide in a manner never before seen. Global revival, massive judgments, and incredible persecution will all happen in the last days. In what manner will these events unfold, and what role will the saints have in this final chapter of human history?

The years before Jesus returns will feature a dramatic clash between demonically inspired kings of the earth and the Praying Church. God will demonstrate the superiority of His strength and wisdom through the saints. His divine judgments will be released because of the intercessory cries of His people. Thus, the full consummation of history will come as a result of the unified prayers of His Bride.

Satan will rage against believers and make war on the saints. God will release judgment events that will pound the planet. In that hour, the Church will find herself vulnerable. Defenseless, naturally speaking, she will be compelled into prayer. God will make use of the less than favorable earthly circumstances to cause His people to call upon His name. The only option for the Church in that day will be prayer. God will remove all of the props she relies on for comfort in order to see the Bride refined as by fire. Ultimately, she will emerge pure, spotless, and leaning on her Beloved.[1]

Prayer: The Catalyst and Response

This day of testing will come as a response to the requests of the Church praying for their King to return. And, in perfect irony, the Lord has seen to it that the only way to make it through this time will be through prayer. Fervent prayer will be both the catalyst and the essential response to the climax of this age.

The eighth chapter of the book of Revelation clearly portrays how the saints' prayers will work to initiate endtime events. An angel with a golden censer mixes all the prayers of the saints together with holy fire and hurls the mixture to the earth. The saints' prayers, mingled with fire, release God's holy judgments. A third of the earth's trees are then burned, along with all the grass. A third of the fresh waters and a third of the sea become poisoned; the sun, moon, and stars are affected. Famine and war grip the planet as death freely runs its course, and men faint from fear. This dark day is the precursor to the birthing of the kingdom on earth; and the entire scenario is brought about by the saints crying out in agreement with God's will.

---

[1]   Song 8:5; Eph. 5:27; 1 Pet. 1:19.

Taking part in the administration of God's divine judgment affords the Praying Church an intimacy not granted to the rest of humanity. Jesus desires to rule and reign with His Bride (Rev. 1:5–6, 20:4). How amazing it is that He actually shares His government with His beloved! Our companionship with Him gives us authority in the heavenly courts of God's kingdom.

Not only do the saints *initiate* the Day of the Lord through prayer; they actually *hasten* its arrival. As we commit today to praying in agreement with Jesus, we quicken the day of His coming. Indeed, every prayer in agreement with His will fills the bowls of Revelation 8 and speeds the day of His return.

It is important that the Church learns to be fervent in prayer before the Day of the Lord appears, for prayer will be our only viable response to that hour of crisis. Communion with the Judge, the Man Christ Jesus, will be the Church's sole mode of survival through tribulation. As the drama of human history comes to a crescendo, the Bride of Christ *must* answer the crisis by abandoning herself to the only realistic option: prayer.

In that hour, Christians will draw confidence from their foresight of the impending judgments. Just as prayer releases divine justice on the earth, prayer will also aid the end-time church in evading the effects of the judgment events. Throughout Scripture, God turns His ear to those who cry out to Him in trials. David, Daniel, Peter, Paul, Silas, and John are all men whom God helped when they petitioned Him in times of great need. Although they still suffered, God shortened their trials, minimizing the effects, because of their responses of prayer and fasting. In the same way, He has promised to aid us at the end of the age (Mt. 24:22).

When God's judgment comes upon the earth, rulers will flee and try to hide, but this will not bring them deliverance. Antichrist will attempt to retaliate against God with his own battle plan, besieging Jerusalem with his armies.[2] However, his plans will be completely ineffectual regardless of the zeal with which he carries them out. A life immersed in passionate, fervent prayer will be the only means by which protection, direction, and provision can be obtained.

The Victorious Church at the End of the Age

> The accuser of our brethren, who accused them before our God day and night, has been cast down. And they overcame him by the blood of the Lamb and by the word of their testimony, and they did not love their lives to the death.
>
> —Revelation 12:10–11

Understanding that the Church will be triumphant at the end of the age is crucial to any study of the end times.[3] Without this lens, the believer's approach to the end times will be the opposite of God's intention. God's consistent desire is to give men dominion on the earth—the way He did with Adam. Prayer is the prescribed method for such dominion to be established in the kingdom of God, both now and in the final years of this age.

Contrary to common belief, the Church *will* be victorious throughout the Great Tribulation. Though

---

[2]   Joel 3:2, 12; Zeph. 3:8; Zech. 12:2-3; 14:2; Rev. 16:14.

[3]   For a discussion of why the Church will not be raptured before the tribulation, see Mike Bickle's "Where Is the Church in the Book of Revelation?" at http://www.ihop.org/Publisher/Article.aspx?ID=1000045068.

economically pressed and physically persecuted, the Bride of Christ will overcome hardship by God's sustaining grace. She will live in communion with the One who initiates and administrates the tribulation; thus, she will be granted deliverance through the time of trouble, similar to the way Daniel emerged from the danger of the lion's den. Because God has ordained this great conflict, the Church need not fear. Rather, through prayer, she must draw confidence from her identity as beloved of the Lord, as well as from the fact that God has promised His people victory.[4] Though she lay down her life, even perhaps unto martyrdom, she will overcome Satan's attempts to cause her to lose faith. Jesus promised us that though we may die, we will not be lost (Lk. 21:16–18). We must adopt His vantage point of victory through trials.

Psalm 149 prophesies about a company of people who will release judgment on the nations through prayer, describing this as a great honor.

> Let the high praises of God be in their mouth . . .
> to execute vengeance on the nations . . . to execute
> on them the written judgment—this honor have
> all His saints.
> —Psalm 149:6–9

At the end of the age, the Church will fulfill this prophecy. Though the nations will rage against God and His people, the Church will win this epic war through intercession. Worldly wisdom might consider prayer as the last resort to obtaining victory. But the saints will astonish the earth's inhabitants as God executes vengeance against the nations on behalf of the Church—all as a result of prayer.

---

4 E.g., "to him who overcomes," Rev. 2–3.

Just and True

> Great and marvelous are Your works, Lord God
> Almighty! Just and true are Your ways, O King of
> the saints! Who shall not fear You, O Lord, and
> glorify Your name? For You alone are holy. For all
> nations shall come and worship before You, for
> Your judgments have been manifested.
> —Revelation 15:3–-4

Revelation 15 includes a beautiful portrayal of the
saints' agreement with God's leadership at the end of the
age. After all the judgments are unleashed upon the earth,
the Church will still confess that God is just and true! The
Church will call His works and His ways, which include
His judgments, great and marvelous. Such a testimony,
however, will be ludicrous to the nations, who will be under the fierce judgments of the Lord. Thus, believers will
be the object of incredible scorn and persecution.

Though martyrdom will sweep the earth and physical persecution against the saints will be unprecedented,
God will empower His people with grace to persevere.
With the help and illumination of the Holy Spirit, God's
people will anchor themselves to His faithfulness, proclaiming His justice even amidst the most horrifying circumstances.

The hymns of praise in the book of Revelation exhibit
this future attitude of the Church. Over and over again,
God's people praise and exalt His name even in the midst
of immense tribulation. The Church will be a righteous
remnant agreeing with every aspect of God's divine government in the generation of the Lord's return.

Birthing the Kingdom

Just as birth pangs begin subtly for a woman who is near childbirth, so will the judgment events that will culminate this age. Almost indiscernibly at first, birth pangs begin to prepare the woman's body to deliver her child. The mother wonders, "Could this be it? Am I in labor?" So, too, will judgment events begin to prepare the earth for the end of this age. In childbirth, the pains intensify and become powerful contractions, leaving no mistake that the child is on his way. Likewise, the subtle pains of creation will turn into full-scale labor that will result in Christ's return and the birthing of God's kingdom.

The earth is already experiencing the initial phase of birth pangs. In His perfect wisdom, God will use these trials to cause His Bride throughout the nations to seek Him in night and day prayer. It will be the epitome of counter-culture for the Church to respond positively and prayerfully to the calamities taking place on the earth. The testimony of God's justice and faithfulness will be scarce among the population in those days. The Church will be the sole entity proclaiming His goodness in the midst of massive upheaval.

Unbelievers will respond by accusing and cursing God. He will be portrayed as wicked in His administration—One who causes calamity and curses humanity. Yet God's perfect leadership and mercy will bring the greatest number of people to salvation through the least severe means possible—He will give all the earth a chance to repent before it is too late. He will gather in a great harvest of new saints, remove all areas of compromise from His Bride, and judge the impenitent. This end-time landscape of trial and challenge will be the ideal context in which

He will perfectly execute His will and enthrone His Son.

Playing Our Role

Whether voluntary or involuntary, Jesus will ultimately have the compliance of every individual upon the earth. Scripture declares that *every* knee will bow and *every* tongue will confess that Jesus is Lord (Phil. 2:10–11). Every eye will see Him when He returns (Rev. 1:7), and the Father will give Him the nations as His inheritance (Ps. 2:8). God has given people the liberty to choose partnership with His Son, even now. And prior to Jesus' earthly establishment as King, believers are offered the unique gift of entering into dynamic partnership with His purposes through prayer.

It is our highest privilege and honor to partner with our glorious King by praying in accordance with His will. Furthermore, we are assured of future partnership with Christ. Jesus said that those who overcome will sit with Him upon His throne, ruling the nations in the next age (Rev. 3:21).

In regard to His coming, Jesus warned His disciples not to be caught unaware, but rather to watch and pray for their master's return (Mk. 13:33, 36–37). He was not speaking of idle star-gazing, nor was He speaking of frenzied works. Rather, He was encouraging us to engage with His plans and with His heart, to stay alert and ready through prayer and fasting.

In the parable of the ten virgins, the guests heard the cry, "The Bridegroom is coming!"(Mt. 25:6). Those who had prepared were ready to meet Him, but those who had not were found wanting, and in the end were unable to enter the wedding feast. Those who desire to participate with Jesus at the end of the age must *prepare now* for their role in the coming great drama.

The call is going forth—the Bridegroom is coming! In the next chapter, we will examine how to make ourselves ready for Him by living lifestyles of prayer and fasting, as the prophetess Anna did.

THE ANNA ANOINTING

Now there was one, Anna, a prophetess, the daughter of Phanuel, of the tribe of Asher. She was of a great age, and had lived with a husband seven years from her virginity; and this woman was a widow of about eighty-four years, who did not depart from the temple, but served God with fastings and prayers night and day. And coming in that instant she gave thanks to the Lord, and spoke of Him to all those who looked for redemption in Jerusalem.

—Luke 2:36–38

We know Anna from her appearance in Luke when she holds the baby Jesus. It is no accident that this woman held the Messiah. Anna didn't just happen to be in the temple that day—she led a lifestyle of continual prayer and fasting, interceding for Israel's Messiah to come. Anna models the life choices necessary to watch and pray. Just as her prayers hastened the first coming, so our prayers can hasten the second coming.

A Day Like No Other

What was it like when Anna came face to face with God in the flesh? Imagine the sense of wonder and awe that Anna must have felt the moment she realized that over sixty years of fasting and prayer had finally seen their fulfillment. She was peering into the face of the Messiah. What was happening in her heart and mind at this stunning revelation that would alter the entire course of human history? To get a clearer picture of Anna's journey, we must consider where it began.

Anna got married as a young woman. According to the International Standard Bible Encyclopedia, "Tradition says that the tribe of Asher was noted for the beauty and talent of its women, who for these gifts, were qualified for royal and high-priestly marriage."[1] It is likely that Anna was a very beautiful and gifted young lady. It is also likely that she had married a notable young man, who was probably well-esteemed and equally gifted. She had been chaste, for she was a virgin when she married. For seven years, she enjoyed the blessings of married life with her husband. Then, the unthinkable happened. Tragedy struck. Her beloved husband passed away. The Bible gives us no information as to his cause of death. All we know is that while Anna was still young and had a life full of promise ahead of her, she was left a widow. How would this young woman emotionally and mentally cope with this catastrophe? What possible life choices could offer her anything close to the bliss she had experienced in her short married life with her husband?

In the moment of her greatest crisis, Anna made an

[1]   *International Standard Bible Encyclopedia*, "Anna," BibleHistory.com, http://www.bible-history.com/isbe/A/ANNA.

amazing and wise decision. Rather than pursuing other options, she determined to devote herself to fasting and prayer. She wholeheartedly pursued God to such an extent that it was said of her that she never left the temple. In the most destructive, pivotal, and challenging time of her life, she made the wisest decision one can make. She gave herself to prayer, clinging to God and God alone.

It is remarkable that Anna's decision was not simply a momentary impulse, for her choice shaped the rest of her life. She found herself in the place of prayer for a year and then two. Two years turned into five, five turned to ten, ten to twenty, and then into many more. This radical, persistent life of abandoning herself to prayer and fasting led to the day in which she found herself peering into the face of the Son of God.

Anna's heritage reflects her journey. She was the daughter of Phanuel, whose name literally means "face of God." Anna's name literally means "grace."[2] Allegorically speaking, it could be said that Anna's journey led her on a collision course by the grace of God to see the face of God.

We know that God does nothing in the earth unless He reveals it to His servants, the prophets (Amos 3:7). Anna was a prophetess, which meant she moved in the realm of the Spirit of God, including experiencing power encounters and receiving supernatural revelation. It is likely that Anna knew by prophetic insight that her constant intercession would culminate in the revelation of Messiah to the earth. I believe that she had "seen" the day many times in her spirit, yet now she was experiencing it with her natural eyes. Perhaps as she came into the

---

[2]   See "Phanuel" and "Anna" at NetBible (http://net.bible.org/dictionary.).

temple that wonderful day, everything seemed strangely familiar. Her mind raced as she asked herself, "Could this be the day?" She rounded the corner to see what she had seen in her heart many times before, yet this time it was happening in front of her—Simeon was prophesying over the baby, the God-man, Jesus. The entire purpose of her life climaxed in that moment.

From that moment forward, she told all who were looking for redemption in Jerusalem about Messiah. Some scholars believe that she actually went door to door throughout all Israel proclaiming to any who would listen that Messiah had come in the flesh.

A Prophetic Picture

This remarkable woman's life is a prophetic picture for the Church today. Just as God released grace upon Anna to fast and pray unto the first physical revelation of Jesus on earth, God is releasing a similar grace upon a whole generation of believers who will operate in a similar anointing, interceding for the next revelation of Jesus on the earth—His second coming. God is igniting a global prayer movement that will usher in the greatest revival, along with the greatest tribulation the world has ever seen, culminating in the return of His Son. In that hour, believers will engage in lives of prayer in the same spirit as Anna.

Anna operated in a unique, three-fold anointing. First, she was clearly an intercessor. She "served God with fastings and prayers, night and day" (Lk. 2:37). It is important to note that the Lord identified Anna's *lifestyle* of fasting and prayer as valid service to Him. Fasting and prayer were part of her regular life of intimacy and devotion to the Lord. Anna had given herself to hearing God's heart and praying His desires back to Him. In fact, prayer is simply hearing the heartbeat of God and asking Him to do what He already wants to do.

Next, Anna operated as a prophetess. Being a prophet does not only mean that one has an anointing in revelatory gifts. It also includes moving in *all* the realms of the Spirit of God, with signs, wonders, and miracles. We can infer that Anna had both a revelatory and a power ministry.

Thirdly, Anna was also clearly an evangelist. Remember that once Anna saw the Lord Jesus, she "spoke of Him to all those who looked for redemption in Jerusalem" (Lk. 2:38). She had drawn close to the Lord in partnership with His heart through fasting and prayer, and had moved in the power of the Holy Spirit. After she saw Jesus, God released authority upon her to proclaim the gospel.

In the earth today, God is raising up a company of believers with a similar three-fold grace and anointing. This generation transcends age and gender; it includes both male and female, young and old. These are people who will give themselves to fasting and prayer as a lifestyle. As Anna did, they will make the wisest choice in the hour of the earth's greatest trial. They will choose prayer in the midst of judgment events and persecution. They will give themselves to prayer and fasting to see God's face revealed with power when Jesus returns to the earth.

Like Anna, these people will operate in every realm of the Spirit of God. They are the prophetic generation of which Joel prophesied—an entire company upon whom God will pour out His Spirit (Joel 2:28-32). These believers will give themselves in abandonment and intimacy to the Lord, and will be filled with the fullness of God (Eph.

3:19). They will manifest the power of the kingdom, moving in signs, wonders, and miracles, and will see the great harvest of souls at the end of the age.

Finally, this generation will be broken for the lost. They will be filled with zeal to proclaim the word of the Lord to all who will listen. With thunder in their mouths, these messengers will authoritatively declare the reality of the risen Christ. The Spirit of the Lord will be upon them as upon no other generation in history. They will fast and pray, preach and prophesy. And the result will be God releasing His power in the earth, gathering untold millions into His kingdom.

Calling Forth the Annas

A young man once said to me, "I think I've got it. It's not fasting *or* prayer, its fasting *and* prayer." I agreed. Anna clearly understood this, and she has become a hero to all who have given themselves to fasting and prayer as the main pursuit of their lives. Her example continues to bring courage to those who yearn to live lifestyles of fasting and prayer and to powerfully proclaim the gospel. God is stirring the hearts of many right now to make radical life decisions, as Anna did. He is calling for prayer and fasting to be the main priority in their lives. Those who will give themselves to this lifestyle will manifest dramatic kingdom power in the earth.

While Anna's trial was personal, the trials that are coming on the earth will be global in scope and far worse in magnitude, testing all who dwell on the earth (Lk. 21:35; Rev. 3:10). We are living in an hour in which the Lord is calling forth the Annas without regard to age or gender, appointing them to fast and pray for the lost. He is bringing them into intimate partnership with His heart to operate as Anna did. Just as Anna's intercession resulted in the first coming of the Lord Jesus, I believe this end-time assembly of Annas will culminate in the return of the Lord Jesus.

If you feel a stirring in your heart towards this lifestyle, it is likely the Lord is calling you to make the same type of decision that Anna made. In this season of mounting turmoil in the earth, an alarm is sounding, calling believers to fast and pray, by God's grace, as their main vocation. Like Anna, you may have an invitation to spend the rest of your days on this earth interceding for the second coming. I believe that we have a short window of time in which to respond to the Spirit's call to watch and pray. Will you respond with abandonment to the Spirit's invitation?

THE JOEL 2 MANDATE

"Turn to Me with all your heart, with fasting, with weeping, and with mourning." So rend your heart, and not your garments; return to the LORD your God, for He is gracious and merciful, slow to anger, and of great kindness; and He relents from doing harm.

—Joel 2:12–13

The Anna lifestyle of prayer and fasting does not merely have personal implications. It is related to a wider reality—the unsaved nations of the earth. Although Anna was ready for the first coming, her nation was not, and many rejected their Messiah. Judgment came upon Israel in 70 AD as the Romans besieged Jerusalem and destroyed the temple. Today, Christians are in a similar position. The Lord will not hold His peace forever against the nations. We must respond not only with individual prayer, but also with focused corporate fasting and intercession.

The book of Joel is invaluable at this time in history, as the world's turmoil deepens and many people rebel against God. Joel gives us a biblical template of God's prescribed lifestyle for people who have rejected His ways and thus are facing His judgment. Joel portrays powerful truths, not only dealing with Israel's history, but also concerning the future Day of the Lord that will affect the whole earth.

The Prophetic Plague

In the first chapter of Joel, the prophet described a plague of locusts that had completely destroyed the land, leaving Israel reeling from its devastating affects. Western readers do not comprehend the destructive power of a locust plague. Imagine a swarm of locusts appears with the haunting hum and buzzing of beating wings. The swarm darkens the sky and causes a pseudo-eclipse as the hordes of insects blot out the rays of the sun. As they devour the crops, they sound like a raging fire devouring a forest. Even more frightening than their appearance is the devastation that they leave in their wake. A swarm of locusts can number in the millions and cover hundreds of square miles of land. A single swarm eats thousands of tons of food daily, easily denuding an entire region.

However, it was not merely one swarm of locusts that was released upon Israel in Joel's day; there were four successive waves. Each continued to pummel the land until the devastation reached a level previously unthinkable. The land was completely ravaged. The crops and the stores of food were destroyed, leaving the nation with no grain or oil. In addition to being part of the staple diet, both grain and oil were offered in the temple, and oil lamps provided light at night.

Imagine how Israel's society was affected as the food and energy supplies were completely cut off. Offerings had to cease in the temple. With a deeply depleted water supply and a decimated food supply, the livestock began to starve to death. To make matters worse, a drought came upon the land. The scorching heat of the sun began to cause brush fires, which consumed the stubble that the locusts had left.

The only possible remedy for this massive ecological crisis was for the land to be drenched in showers of refreshing rain. God promised He would pour out rain upon Israel's dry land if His people would turn to Him with all their hearts.

In chapter 2, Joel told the people to sound an alarm and gather the multitudes together for a solemn assembly of fasting and prayer. Joel urged the Israelites to repent and turn back to the Lord with all their hearts so that God would heal their land.

The Ultimate Judgment

Joel then stunned his hearers with a shocking word from the Lord. The chilling message was this: Though the locust plague was extremely severe, it was not the final judgment. He told them that the locust plague was only a prophetic picture of the *real* judgment that would come upon them if they did not return to the Lord. He said that an exceedingly fierce and destructive army was coming— the Babylonians.

They were well known for the massive destruction that they brought upon the surrounding nations. As they conquered neighboring lands, they tortured and murdered the people and burned their cities to the ground. They were the most feared and savage military force of that day.

Joel told the Israelites that just as the locusts had

destroyed the land, the Babylonians would devour Israel and incinerate everything in their path; that they had undergone an introductory measure of judgment, but that a greater judgment was approaching. The only way to avert it was for God's people to assemble in fasting, prayer, and repentance. He urged them to call a solemn assembly, to rend their hearts, return to the Lord, and escape judgment.

The people entered into a season of repentance and revival after the preaching of Joel, and God brought healing to the land (during the reign of King Josiah). However, their repentance was spiritually shallow and short-lived. They soon returned to their idol worship and rebellion. Their refusal to heed the warnings of Joel and other prophets eventually brought upon them the very judgment the Lord had decreed. The Babylonian army swept down upon Jerusalem in three different waves, conquering it in less than twenty years.

Babylon completely decimated the land, destroying their homes and the temple, and scattering the people. The sad fact is that Israel did not have to experience this judgment. If the people had turned to the Lord with their whole hearts, the Lord would have relented.

When God sends messengers to warn His people and the people do not heed those warnings, God's only choice is to release judgment. He does this because of the covenant He has with His people. He will not allow them to continue in their sin, but will do whatever is necessary to get their attention so that they turn their hearts back towards Him.

The Plagues of Our Generation

The book of Joel should be an unsettling warning to

us in this generation. Many people focus on the promise of the outpouring of the Spirit when they read Joel (Joel 2:28–32). But they are almost completely unaware that this promised end-time outpouring is going to come as a stroke of mercy just *before* the great and terrible Day of the Lord—God's ultimate judgment upon the earth. The Day of the Lord will shake the whole earth to bring vindication to the righteous and retribution to the wicked (2 Thes. 1:6–10).

Joel's prophecies have not yet been completely fulfilled. The fearsome words of chapters 2 and 3 proclaim that a season of global judgment against all the nations is coming. God raised up the Babylonian army as an instrument of judgment against Israel. This is a prophetic picture of the future army that is coming at the end of the age—an army that will be led by Antichrist himself. God will use him as an instrument of judgment just as He used the Babylonians (and other invaders throughout Israel's history). Antichrist will devour the nations and demand that the people worship him as god. This coming day will be the greatest day of tribulation the earth has ever seen.

In this present generation, we have watched sin escalate to a proportion the world has never seen before. We live in the first generation in which the wholesale murder of infants is acceptable and protected by law in many parts of the world. We live in a time in which millions of people are held as slaves,[1] exploited sexually and for their labor— more than at any other time in the history of the world. Homosexuality has been embraced as an alternative lifestyle. Pornography is available on-demand through the vehicle of the Internet. Biblical signs of the end of the age are being fulfilled before our very eyes.

[1] Estimates from varying sources range from 12 million to 30 million.

For instance, in the United States, we claim to be a nation "under God." Yet it is obvious that we have greatly strayed from the foundational truths of Christianity. It has become commonplace in the Church to pursue large crowds and the praise of men while ignoring the core values of the kingdom of God, such as meekness, mercy, and hunger for righteousness. We are concerned with becoming "relevant" to a wicked world, rather than being the light of the world and the salt of the earth. If we are, as Jesus put it, salt without its flavor (Mt. 5:13), how can we be effective in transforming the lives of the lost?

Because of the state of our nation and, more importantly, the state of the *Church* in our nation, America stands in danger of significant judgment. We have effectively signed up for God's judgment by slaughtering babies, embracing homosexuality, and becoming the world's largest purveyor of perversion and pornography. Yet the Church is asleep. Let us not forget that, as of this writing, we are only eight years removed from the catastrophe of 9/11, and just four years from the tragic events of hurricane Katrina which rendered the entire Gulf Coast of the United States powerless. The first wave of locusts has begun to descend upon us, and we are oblivious to the fact that destruction has come and is still coming. We live in a state of spiritual delusion. We are intoxicated by our religiosity, yet we have little evidence of an authentic faith. We compromise our Christian walk by being intertwined with the world, yet we believe that we are safe and secure in our salvation. How we need a true witness of the gospel that turns the hearts of the masses to the Lord!

How Then Shall We Live?

Our only hope is to embrace the lifestyle outlined in Joel 2. I believe a trumpet is sounding in the Spirit right now. It is calling us to return to the Lord through fasting and prayer, weeping and mourning. We must repent fully and turn to the Lord with all our hearts. Then we will see the spiritual darkness that has possessed our nation overthrown and revival released. Joel 2 is clear: solemn assemblies devoted to fasting, prayer, and repentance are the only antidote for the judgments that are sure to come upon our nation—indeed, any nation.

As we have discussed, God is raising up companies of believers throughout the earth who are gathering together in ceaseless intercession. The most productive and biblically sound way to address the issues that we face in our day is through fasting, prayer, and repentance. When communities gather together under the banner of Joel 2 and engage in night and day prayer, they are in essence living in a perpetual solemn assembly. A lifestyle of continual prayer and fasting is the only answer to the dark conditions of our nation; it is essential for a spiritual shift to ensue. If we embrace Joel 2 as an end-time mandate, God will hear our cries, have mercy on our sin, and release a great move of His Spirit.

Some may ask, "How practical is it to live a *lifestyle* of fasting and prayer?" For some, being a part of a perpetual solemn assembly might mean connecting with a community of believers who take turns as watchmen on the wall. Some may have jobs that occupy much of their day, but will still do their part, praying alongside fellow believers two, five, ten, or more hours per week. Others will give themselves full-time to the cause, making prayer and worship their vocation. Throughout the earth, many people are being commissioned by the Lord to serve Him in fasting and prayer as their vocation, just as the Levites of old and Anna did.

Who Can Stand?

The probing question the book of Joel asks is, "For the day of the Lord is great and very terrible; who can endure it?"(Joel 2:11). A great shaking is coming to the earth (Hag 2:21–22). Who will be able to stand? The Joel 2 lifestyle is the key to being able to endure in that day. When we give ourselves to fasting and prayer, and in tenderness turn our hearts to the Lord, God will hear our cries and release mercy to us. He not only *loves* mercy; His very *name* is mercy (Ex. 34:6).

Whether you pray two hours a week or fifty, being a part of a community of believers who seek the Lord continually through prayer and fasting is essential in light of the impending judgments. Scripture is clear that many will fall away during the time of great crisis (2 Thes. 2:3; 1 Tim. 4:1). Ultimately, those who stand firm at the end of the age will love truth and be given to prayer. The spotless Bride for whom Jesus will return will be a praying Church (Rev. 22:17).

Can You Hear the Sound?

The question for us now is, "Will the Church heed the call to fast and pray?" Will we hear the alarm that is being sounded in the Spirit, calling us to embrace the Joel 2 mandate? Can we hear the sound of the locust wings beginning to hum? Will we perceive the darkness that has begun to cover us? The catastrophes that we have seen in the last several years are only the beginning of what is coming. But as we give ourselves to prayer and fasting, God will answer with mercy and release the promised end-time outpouring of His Spirit that will literally sweep millions into His kingdom.

Night and day prayer affords us the opportunity of living our lives in consistent fasting, prayer, worship, and repentance—to intercede for the kingdom to come and the Bride to be ready. While many may have strategies for church growth or "relevant outreaches," these strategies are not going to stem the tide of the judgment that is coming upon our nation. The Joel 2 mandate is vital to the global prayer movement, uniting believers in a cry for mercy. The alarm is sounding and we must heed the call!

There is still hope for us. The greatest move of God's Spirit is yet to come. My prayer is that the Church would heed the call to fast and pray night and day, that we would see the spiritual climate shift and mercy pour down upon us. God will come to us like rain if we will return to Him with all of our heart (Hos. 6:3). Will you heed the call to fast and pray until He comes?

IHOP Atlanta MISSIONS BASE

On February 12, 2006, a prayer and worship meeting began in Atlanta that continues to this very hour. Since that day, night and day worship and intercession have continually ascended to the throne of God from Atlanta. Convinced that Jesus is worthy of ceaseless worship, men and women of all ages are giving themselves to lives of extravagant devotion expressed through 24/7 prayer. Structured in eighty-four 2-hour prayer meetings per week, full teams of musicians, singers, and intercessors lift their voices in praise and supplication, asking God to fulfill His promise and give the nations of the earth to Jesus as His inheritance.

IHOP–Atlanta is a ministry serving the entire metro-Atlanta area, open twenty-four hours a day for any person or group desiring to come at any time to worship and pray individually or corporately. The prayer room is the heartbeat of all that goes on at the IHOP–Atlanta Missions Base. Each prayer meeting follows one of four formats: devotional worship, prophetic worship, worship with the Word, or intercession.

Visiting IHOP–Atlanta

One-day Seminars: These intense one-day trainings are held on the first Saturday of each month. Topics of study include "Growing in the Spirit of Prophecy," "Omega—Studies in the End Times," "Passion for Jesus," and "The Harp and Bowl Model of Worship and Intercession." Registration is available online at www.ihop-atlanta.com.

Encounter Services: Services are held every Sunday at 10:00am and 6:00pm. The IHOP–Atlanta Encounter Service is a unique gathering that provides an atmosphere of freedom of worship, instruction, and exhortation from the Word, as well as prophetic impartation. Each service incorporates prophetic worship, biblical teaching, prayer, and ministry times. These weekly times of encounter are heavily dependent on the grace and leading of the Holy Spirit. Each service is geared towards calling individuals to a depth of the knowledge of God, intimacy with Jesus, urgency for the hour, and the Sermon on the Mount lifestyle.

Internships

The goal of the International House of Prayer–Atlanta internships is to equip individuals in the messages of intimacy with Jesus, urgency for the hour, and the Sermon on the Mount lifestyle. Each internship affords the individual the opportunity to live in the environment of night and day prayer as an intercessory missionary with structured times of fasting and prayer, outreach, instruction, and impartation.

Intro: A three-month, daytime training program for all ages, married or single.

The Watch Internship: A three-month internship for ages 18-30 taking place during the NightWatch, from midnight to 6:00am.

The Pursuit Internship: A three-month daytime internship for young adults ages 18-25.

The Nitro Internship: A three-month internship for married couples and singles taking place during the NightWatch, from midnight to 6:00am.

The Joshua Internship: A three-month daytime internship for adults 50 and older.

Encounter Teen Camp: A one-week program held each summer to equip teens in prophetic worship, intercession, and intimacy with Jesus.

Gatekeeper School of Ministry

Gatekeeper School of Ministry is a part-time ministry school focused on equipping forerunners with urgency for the hour and intimacy with God. Intimacy and urgency release profound conviction for the necessity of night and day worship and prayer. Students are challenged to approach the Word of God with a collegiate academic zeal, while maintaining a devotional spirit bathed in the atmosphere of 24/7 worship and intercession. In this unique environment, revelation of the Word goes deep into the heart causing the student to grow in the knowledge of God. Three 12-week trimesters are offered annually.

Visit the IHOP–Atlanta Website for more information:

WWW.IHOP-ATLANTA.COM

Podcasts, MP3 Downloads, Prayer Room Blogs, Internship Applications, Seminar Registration, School of Ministry, Upcoming Events, Conferences, and More . . .

International House of Prayer
Missions Base

....

24/7 Live Worship and Prayer
IHOP.org

....

Since September 19, 1999, we have continued in night and day prayer with worship as the foundation of our ministry to win the lost, heal the sick, and make disciples as we labor alongside the larger Body of Christ to see the Great Commission fulfilled and to function as forerunners who prepare the way for the return of Jesus. By the grace of God, we are committed to combining 24/7 prayers for justice with 24/7 works for justice until the Lord returns. We do this best as our lives are rooted in prayer that focuses on intimacy with God and intercession for breakthrough of the fullness of God's power and purpose for this generation.

For more information on our internships, conferences, university, live prayer room webcast, and more, please visit our website at IHOP.org.

International House of Prayer Missions Base of Kansas City
3535 E. Red Bridge Road, Kansas City, MO 64137
816.763.0200 • info@ihop.org • IHOP.org

IHOPU

International House of Prayer University

....

Ministry, Music, Media, and eSchool
IHOP.org/university

....

The International House of Prayer University (IHOPU) is a full-time Bible school which exists to equip this generation in the knowledge of God and the power of the Spirit for the bold proclamation of the Lord Jesus and His return.

Students embrace rigorous theological training and Sermon on the Mount lifestyles in the context of a thriving missions base fueled by night and day prayer (IHOP–KC). As a result, theological education obtained in the classroom is intrinsically connected to intimacy with Jesus and hands-on experience.

IHOPU is distinct from many other institutions of higher learning in the United States in that we seek a holistic approach to education with an emphasis on the forerunner ministry, and a NightWatch training element. IHOPU is led by intercessory missionaries in an environment of night and day prayer and a thriving missions base.

International House of Prayer University
3535 E. Red Bridge Road, Kansas City, MO 64137
816.763.0243 • ihopu@ihop.org • IHOP.org/university